# THE FOUNDATIONS OF EFFECTIVE COACHING

A BLUEPRINT FOR BUILDING TRUST, LEADING BY EXAMPLE, AND CREATING LASTING SUCCESS IN THE FITNESS INDUSTRY

WADE MERRILL

# CONTENTS

*Introduction: Bridging the Gap*      5

1. Bridging the Learning Gap      13
2. Building Trust: The Foundation of Coaching      21
3. Communicating Effectively      41
4. The Coach's Mindset      67
5. The Client Journey      87
6. Showing Up for Yourself as a Coach      103
7. The Coach's Legacy      117
   Epilogue: The Journey Ahead      129

*References*      135

# INTRODUCTION: BRIDGING THE GAP

The first year of a personal trainer's career often feels like being thrown into the deep end without a life preserver. New trainers, brimming with excitement and ambition, step into the fitness industry ready to change lives. But they quickly encounter a reality far more complex than they imagined. The role isn't just about programming workouts or correcting form—it's about building trust, navigating relationships, adapting to challenges, and cultivating the mindset to lead with confidence and empathy.

For many, the transition from certification to real-world coaching is overwhelming. The gap between knowing what to do and knowing how to do it effectively is wide. Without guidance or mentorship, even the most promising trainers can lose their footing. From what I've witnessed, the majority of trainers leave the industry within their first year, disillusioned by the emotional, physical, and professional demands of the job. Promising careers fade, and the industry loses untapped potential daily—not because trainers lack talent, but because they lack the tools and support to thrive.

But it doesn't have to be this way.

## MY FIRST SESSION: A HUMBLING START

When I was 19, I stepped into my first official role as a personal trainer at Lifetime Fitness. I had spent two years preparing—studying at the National Personal Training Institute, practicing with peers, and even training friends and classmates for free. I felt ready to take on paying clients, confident that my knowledge and passion would carry me through. But my first session taught me a lesson I wasn't prepared for.

My client was a 65-year-old woman who had never exercised before. She was obese, a former smoker, and lived on one meal a day—typically a business lunch or dinner. She had tried countless diets with no lasting success and finally decided to give strength training a try. She signed up for three sessions a week for three months.

I was so eager to help that I approached her session like I was training a seasoned athlete. After a brief cardiovascular assessment, I entered her biometric data into Lifetime's system, calculated her "body age," and jumped straight into a program I believed was appropriate for any beginner:

- 3 sets of leg press
- 3 sets of leg extension

- 3 sets of machine chest press
- 3 sets of machine rows

I congratulated her at the end of the session, warned her she might feel some soreness, and sent her on her way. I was sure I'd done everything right.

I was wrong.

Four days later, she returned, barely able to walk. She was in so much pain that she couldn't move comfortably for days. She was understandably upset and felt betrayed by someone she had trusted to help her—not hurt her. My heart sank as she told my manager what had happened. I had underestimated her starting point and pushed her far beyond what her body could handle. My eagerness to prove myself had caused me to fail her.

That moment changed everything for me. I realized that coaching isn't about showing clients what you know—it's about meeting them where they are, building trust, and guiding them forward with care and intention.

## THE CHALLENGE OF GROWTH

Looking back, that experience was a turning point. I learned that being a personal trainer isn't just about acquiring knowledge—it's about applying it effectively. Growth as a coach means showing up every day with humility, curiosity, and the willingness to improve. It's about embracing your journey of development while helping your clients navigate theirs.

The truth is, the fitness industry doesn't offer new trainers the same support systems found in other professions. Doctors have residencies. Teachers have student teaching. What about trainers? They're left to figure it out on their own. Without mentorship or structured guidance, many adopt a "fake it till you make it" mentality—projecting confidence while quietly struggling to stay afloat.

This approach might seem practical in the short term, but it often leads to burnout and stagnation. Growth requires vulnerability—the courage to acknowledge gaps in your knowledge, seek feedback, and continually adapt.

## WHY I WROTE THIS BOOK

This book is the resource I wish I'd had when I was starting out. It's not about quick fixes or shortcuts—it's about building a sustainable coaching mindset rooted in growth, empathy, and leadership. Each chapter is designed to help you navigate the real challenges you'll face as a trainer, from building client trust to staying motivated during your own struggles.

But at its core, this book is about something bigger than you or me: it's about learning to serve our clients better. It's about creating the kind of fluid morale that seamlessly adapts to each person—with the right energy, the right emotional tone, and the right words. It's about developing a presence that inspires trust, a professionalism that commands respect, and an environment where clients feel empowered to grow. I call that *the coach's mindset*.

I've observed trainers who could captivate a room with just their voice. I've seen the impact of a coach who deeply cares for their clients' well-being, so much so that they continuously work to level themselves up—not out of obligation, but out of an unwavering commitment to guide and develop others. That's the vision I want to share with you.

What this book is *not* is a technical manual guaranteeing you success if you read it. You won't find sales training, program design, or coaching techniques here. Those have their place, but this book focuses on something deeper: the spirit of coaching. It's about the kind of mindset and daily approach that the trainers who want to be great must adopt.

Over the course of 20 years, I've seen the full spectrum of what the fitness industry has to offer. I've witnessed moments of selfishness, deception, and disrespect, but I've also worked alongside incredible people—trainers and coaches whose integrity, dedication, and professionalism have inspired me. These individuals are proof that the fitness industry is capable of something greater, something extraordinary.

I believe we can fill this industry with professionally minded leaders who carry themselves with unwavering integrity. Leaders who inspire trust, elevate those around them, and set a new standard for what coaching can and should be. When I think of great leaders, the word that comes to mind is *sacrifice*. How much are they willing to give to serve something bigger than themselves? The next word is *meekness*—the ability to recognize when to take a stand, when to step back, and when to simply observe. True leaders are everywhere—ready to lead, ready to follow, ready to put in the work, and wise enough to recharge when needed.

When I think of great coaches, I see someone fully engaged with their client in every detail of their craft during a training session. From monitoring the quality of reps to timing their client's breathing, observing their recovery, and listening intently—these coaches are learners while they lead. They assess, adjust, and improve not only their clients' performance but also their own approach, session after session.

This book is for the trainers who want more—for themselves, for their clients, and for the industry as a whole. My hope is that it helps you embody the principles of sacrifice, humility, and unwavering commitment to your craft. Together, we can forge a new standard of excellence in fitness coaching.

## A PROMISE TO YOUNG TRAINERS

Over the past 20 years, I've learned that creating meaningful change isn't just about helping clients reach their goals—it's about growing as a coach, a leader, and a person. But this book isn't about me. It's about you. Whether you're just starting your journey or searching for a spark to reignite your passion, this book is here to guide you.

I don't have all the answers, and I'm not pretending to. This book isn't a final word—it's a reflection of my perspective, my experiences, and the lessons I've learned so far. It's not meant to reflect every coach's journey, nor should it. Instead, consider it an invitation to pause, reflect, and grow. You don't need to have it all figured out right now. What matters most is your willingness to show up, to learn, and to take that next step forward.

The fitness industry needs more professionals who lead with meekness—strength guided by wisdom—and with unwavering integrity. My hope is that this book provides you with the tools, perspective, and encouragement to not just build a career, but to create a legacy of service, growth, and excellence.

Let's lay the foundation together.

1

# BRIDGING THE LEARNING GAP

## THE FIRST STEPS

The first steps of any trainer's career are often filled with equal parts excitement and uncertainty. You've earned your certification, stepped into the gym, and are eager to make a difference. But then reality sets in. Clients aren't just looking for workouts—they're looking for guidance, connection, and trust. Suddenly, you realize that what you learned in your certification courses only scratches the surface of what it takes to truly lead others.

For many trainers, this is where the learning gap emerges. The technical knowledge you've gained is valuable, but it doesn't prepare you for the deeper, more nuanced aspects of coaching: building trust, navigating communication, and adapting to the emotional and physical needs of each client. This gap can feel overwhelming, and without support, it's easy to fall into patterns that hinder growth.

## THE LEARNING GAP IN COACHING

The fitness industry thrives on the principle of leadership. As trainers, you're expected to guide, motivate, and inspire your clients. But leadership isn't something you earn with a certification or a job title—it's a skill set and a mindset that must be cultivated over time. While a job title may grant you authority, true leadership is earned through action, education, and experience—and ultimately, it's accepted by those who trust and depend on you.

There's often a significant gap between the day you receive your certification and the day you feel like a confident, effective professional. During this period, many adopt a "fake it till you make it" mentality, focusing on projecting competence rather than addressing their struggles head-on.

While this approach may seem practical, it can be counterproductive. Ignoring challenges doesn't make them disappear; it allows them to fester. Over time, unresolved struggles can hinder your growth, compromise client relationships, and limit your impact as a coach.

## THE MISSING PIECE: MENTORSHIP

In professions where leadership is central, mentorship is often the linchpin of development. Leaders learn from other leaders—they receive guidance, feedback, and accountability to refine their skills. Yet, in the fitness industry, mentorship is surprisingly rare. Trainers are often left to figure it out on their own, managing client relationships, building trust, and navigating the emotional toll of the role without guidance.

This lack of mentorship creates a void. Without a trusted mentor to offer constructive feedback and model effective coaching, many trainers struggle to develop the skills they need to succeed. Instead of growing into their potential, they stall, recycle ineffective habits, and, in many cases, burn out. Promising trainers often leave the fitness industry before they ever see their full potential or experience the rewards of this great career path.

## SELF-CRITIQUE: THE PATH TO GROWTH

The absence of mentorship doesn't mean growth is impossible—it simply means it's harder. For trainers committed to excellence, self-critique becomes essential.

Growth requires honesty about your weaknesses, even when it feels uncomfortable. This isn't about tearing yourself down—it's about taking an honest look at what's working, what's not, and how you can improve.

A good mentor naturally provides this perspective, highlighting blind spots and encouraging progress. In the absence of a mentor, you must take ownership of this process yourself. Ask reflective questions like:

- *What are my strengths as a coach?*
- *Where do I struggle to connect with clients?*
- *What's one thing I can focus on improving this week?*

While self-reflection can feel counterintuitive—it's far easier to avoid discomfort than to lean into it—it's a critical step in your development. The most effective coaches are those who embrace this process, seeking feedback even from their clients and committing to continual improvement.

## THE COST OF AVOIDING GROWTH

I've seen the consequences of avoiding growth firsthand. Some trainers fall into a one-size-fits-all approach, treating every client the same regardless of their needs. Others let stress and frustration seep into their sessions, unintentionally signaling to clients that they're an afterthought. I'll never forget a trainer I worked with early in my career who told his clients: *"If you see results, hooray for me. If you don't, shame on you."*

This mindset may protect a trainer's ego, but it damages relationships and undermines the trust needed for lasting success. Coaching isn't about blame or rigid expectations—it's about partnership. It's about meeting clients where they are and guiding them forward with empathy and intention.

## BRIDGING THE GAP BETWEEN AVERAGE AND EXCEPTIONAL

The difference between an average trainer and an exceptional coach isn't certifications or accolades—it's an intentional, self-reflective effort. While technical knowledge and credentials are important, they aren't what create transformative experiences for clients.

Exceptional coaches focus on cultivating qualities that go beyond textbook knowledge:

- **Self-Awareness:** Recognizing how your mood, energy, and actions influence your clients. Every interaction matters, from the tone of your voice to the expressions on your face.
- **Humility:** Acknowledging that sessions are about your clients, not you. Humility means admitting when you don't know something and prioritizing the client's needs over your ego.
- **Empathy:** Meeting clients where they are—emotionally, mentally, and physically. Great coaches understand the barriers their clients face because they care.

These qualities form the foundation of effective coaching. Leadership isn't about being perfect; it's about showing up every day with a commitment to doing better—for yourself, for your clients, and for the industry.

## SETTING A HIGHER STANDARD

The fitness industry often sets a low bar for professionalism. Trainers enter the field without understanding how to present themselves as professionals, relying on what they've seen or what social media dictates. This leads to behaviors that undermine trust and credibility, such as:

- **Disengagement:** Scrolling through phones during sessions or failing to be fully present.
- **Unprofessionalism:** Wearing inappropriate attire or discussing personal issues with clients.
- **Overstepping Boundaries:** Offering advice and guidance on topics outside their expertise.

As coaches, we have a responsibility to set a higher standard—not just for ourselves, but for the industry as a whole. This starts with holding ourselves accountable to professionalism, integrity, and growth.

## BRIDGING THE GAP: WHAT THIS BOOK OFFERS

If you feel stuck in the learning gap—navigating client relationships, adapting to challenges, or finding your footing—this book is here to guide you. It's designed to be the mentor you may not have, equipping you with the mindset, tools, and strategies to thrive as a coach.

Each chapter that follows addresses a critical aspect of coaching, building a roadmap for long-term success:

- **Chapter 2: Building Trust:** The foundation of meaningful coaching relationships that foster client loyalty and progress.
- **Chapter 3: Communicating Effectively:** How to connect with clients through verbal, non-verbal, visual, and tactile communication.

- **Chapter 4: The Coach's Mindset:** Embracing growth, empathy, and leadership to show up fully for your clients and yourself.
- **Chapter 5: The Client Journey:** Adapting programs and strategies to meet clients where they are and guiding them through highs and lows.
- **Chapter 6: Showing Up for Yourself as a Coach:** Prioritizing your well-being, setting boundaries, and cultivating resilience to sustain a fulfilling career.
- **Chapter 7: The Coach's Legacy:** Leaving a lasting impact on clients, colleagues, and the industry through trust, leadership, and influence.

This book isn't about quick fixes or shortcuts—it's about building a sustainable foundation for growth. Each chapter provides actionable tools, reflection exercises, and insights designed to guide you through the challenges of coaching, transforming your approach from good to great.

## A JOURNEY, NOT A DESTINATION

Growth isn't linear, and it won't happen overnight. This book won't give you all the answers, but it will help you ask the right questions, take intentional action, and reflect on what works for you and your clients. Progress is made in small, consistent steps—and those steps start here.

## Reflection Exercises

1. **Identify Your Gaps:** Reflect on areas where you feel least confident as a coach. Write them down and choose one to focus on improving this week.
2. **Seek Feedback:** Ask a trusted client or colleague for feedback. What's one thing they appreciate? What's one thing you could improve?
3. **Set a Growth Goal:** Choose one skill to work on for the next month. Track your progress and celebrate small wins.

## Key Takeaways

- Leadership in coaching is cultivated through self-awareness, humility, and empathy.
- The absence of mentorship creates a gap that trainers must bridge through self-reflection and intentional growth.
- Avoiding growth stalls progress, while embracing feedback accelerates it.

2

# BUILDING TRUST: THE FOUNDATION OF COACHING

Trust is the cornerstone of every successful coaching relationship. It's not something you can demand or assume—it must be earned, moment by moment and session by session. Without trust, even the most expertly designed program will fall short. With trust, clients are more likely to commit fully to the process, share their goals and fears, and push through challenges and setbacks to achieve lasting success.

At one end of building trust lies your personal accountability as a coach. This starts with mastering the fundamental knowledge required to effectively guide your clients. Before you can focus on rapport or empathy, you must first ensure you have the technical expertise to be trusted to deliver results. That means possessing a solid understanding of program design, anatomy, biomechanics, and exercise science. At the very least, you should have earned a recognized certification, such as NASM-

CPT or its equivalent, to demonstrate your foundational competence.

Why is this important? Because everything else in this chapter—the skills, strategies, and qualities that foster trust—rests on the assumption that you're not "winging it." As a fitness professional, your ethical responsibility begins with being qualified to step into this role. Clients place their trust in your ability to lead them safely and effectively toward their goals. Without this baseline, the trust you aim to build will falter, regardless of your best intentions.

But technical knowledge alone isn't enough. Building trust goes beyond simply being competent, friendly, or professional. It's about creating an environment where your clients feel safe, supported, and understood—where they know their journey is as important to you as it is to them. At the heart of building trust lies rapport, the essential connection that sets the tone for everything else.

## WHAT IS RAPPORT?

Rapport is the process of connecting with your clients on a personal level, creating a sense of mutual understanding and comfort. It's about forming a relationship where your client feels valued and respected while you're getting to know them better. Rapport sets the stage for deeper trust and collaboration.

Building rapport isn't something you labor over or try to "get right." It's less about strategy and more about showing up as your authentic, professional self. Think of it as meeting a new friend for coffee—you're naturally curious, you listen, and you find ways to connect over shared experiences or interests. While rapport doesn't require perfection, it does benefit from thoughtfulness.

When you view rapport as an opportunity to connect rather than a task to complete, it becomes a natural extension of your role as a coach. This thoughtful yet easygoing approach helps clients lower their guard, making them more likely to trust and engage with you.

STRATEGIES FOR BUILDING RAPPORT

Here are some brief practical ways to foster rapport with your clients:

*1. Start with Genuine Curiosity*

Show sincere interest in your client's goals, experiences, and concerns by asking open-ended questions. Authenticity isn't optional—it's essential. Clients can sense when a question is asked out of obligation rather than genuine care. Approach every conversation with the intent to truly understand their story and what drives them, not just to check a box or gather surface-level information. For example:

- *"What made you decide to start training?"*
- *"What's one thing you've enjoyed about exercise in the past?"*

## 2. Find Common Ground

Look for shared interests or values, even outside of fitness, to create a personal connection. It could be a love for a sport, a team, a favorite genre of music, or an appreciation for their sense of humor or unique perspective.

## 3. Listen to Understand

Practice active listening by giving your full attention, paraphrasing to confirm understanding, and avoiding interruptions. As Stephen Covey puts it:

> *"Most people do not listen with the intent to understand; they listen with the intent to reply."*

## 4. Show Empathy and Encouragement

Acknowledge your client's challenges and celebrate their wins, no matter how small. Thoughtful encouragement helps clients feel supported and motivated, reinforcing their commitment to the process.

Recognizing and celebrating small successes activates the brain's reward system, releasing dopamine and reinforcing positive behaviors. This neurological response fosters a sense of accomplishment and progress, which boosts both self-efficacy and self-esteem. Over time, these small wins create a positive feedback loop of motivation and satisfaction, making clients more likely to stick with their fitness journey and achieve their goals (Psychology Today, 2024).

Additionally, acknowledging small wins enhances overall satisfaction and well-being, providing a sense of fulfillment that contributes to increased happiness and engagement in both personal and professional aspects of life (AhaSlides, 2024).

By consistently celebrating these milestones, you not only help clients stay on track but also reinforce their belief in their own ability to succeed. This thoughtful, empathetic approach strengthens the coach-client relationship and fosters long-term commitment.

## THE ROLE OF TRUST IN COACHING

Once rapport is established, trust becomes the foundation for a lasting coaching relationship. Without trust, even the best workout program will fall flat. Clients won't fully buy into your guidance if they don't believe in you as a coach. Trust allows for honest communication, productive feedback, and the ability to push through challenges together.

**Building Trust Requires:**

*1. Authenticity*

Trust begins with being real. Authenticity means showing up as your genuine self—no facades, no pretense, just you. Clients can sense when a coach is being insincere, and nothing erodes trust faster than a lack of authenticity. When you are transparent about your intentions, your strengths, and even your imperfections, you show clients that trust is a two-way street.

**To practice authenticity:**

- **Be honest about your expertise and limitations.** For example, if a client asks about a topic outside your scope, don't fabricate an answer. Instead, say, *"That's a great question. Let me research it or connect you with someone who specializes in that area."*
- Admit mistakes and own them. If you misspeak or misstep, acknowledge it. A simple, *"You know what? That wasn't the best way to explain that—let me rephrase,"* reinforces that you are human and committed to improving.
- **Be consistent with your values.** Clients are drawn to coaches whose actions align with their words. Live out the principles you encourage in others.

When you are authentic, you create a space where clients feel safe being themselves, which is the foundation for trust.

*2. Empathy*

Empathy is about meeting clients where they are—emotionally, mentally, and physically. It requires setting aside assumptions and taking the time to truly understand their unique challenges, fears, and motivations. Empathy shows clients that their story matters to you, which deepens trust and connection.

**To Practice Empathy:**

- **Listen to Understand, Not to Respond.** Approach each conversation with the goal of truly hearing your client's concerns, rather than formulating your reply while they're speaking. Resist the urge to interrupt or "fix" their issues immediately. Allow them to fully express themselves before responding, creating a safe space for open dialogue.
- **Reflect and Confirm Understanding.** Use reflective statements to validate their perspective and ensure you're on the same page. For example, *"It sounds like you've been feeling frustrated about [specific challenge]. Is that right?"* This approach not only demonstrates that you're actively listening but also opens the door for them to clarify or expand if needed. If your reflection is slightly off, the phrasing gives space for continued conversation without them feeling misunderstood.
- **Validate their emotions.** Even if you don't share their experience, acknowledge their feelings with empathetic phrases like, *"I know this feels tough, but you're showing a lot of resilience by sticking with it."* This reinforcement builds trust and helps clients feel seen and supported in their journey.

Empathy is not about having all the answers; it's about creating a space where clients feel heard, valued, and supported. This fosters a deeper sense of trust and partnership.

### *3. Patience*

Trust isn't built overnight—it's a process that requires mutual understanding, respect, and time. As a trainer, patience means embracing the client's journey as it unfolds, without rushing results or forcing them to meet milestones that may not align with their unique circumstances.

**Let Their Timeline Guide You:**

- **Develop an Intelligent Plan:** Crafting a structured program that outlines a client's potential progress over 3, 6, 9, or 12 months is an essential part of coaching. This plan provides a roadmap, but it's not a rigid script. The key is to approach it with adaptability, recognizing that life, physical limitations, and unforeseen challenges can affect even the best-designed periodization.
- **Respect Their Progress:** A patient trainer respects the client's ability to progress at their own level. Sometimes their pace will align with your expectations, and sometimes it won't—and that's okay. Your role is to meet them where they are, not where you expect them to be.

- **Be Flexible Together:** Collaboratively adjust the plan as needed, based on their attendance, performance, progress, feedback, and real-life circumstances.
- **Understand Shared Challenges:** Progress isn't always within your control—or theirs. Clients might face injuries, health issues, or life demands that slow their journey. Your patience and understanding during these moments help maintain trust and encourage them to stay engaged.

**Celebrate Incremental Progress:**

Always be sure to celebrate the small wins to reinforce the value of steady effort. Whether it's mastering a movement, staying consistent for a month, or simply showing up on a tough day, these victories remind both you and your client that progress is happening—even if it's not linear.

*4. Consistency:*

Trust thrives on dependability. When you consistently show up on time, follow through on your promises, and prioritize the client's experience, you communicate that they can count on you. Consistency isn't just about being punctual—it's about showing up mentally, emotionally, and physically prepared for every session.

Key practices to build consistency:

- **Set a welcoming tone.** Establish routines that make clients feel seen and valued, such as greeting them warmly or beginning each session with a quick check-in.
- **Follow through.** If you promise to send resources or adjust their program, deliver on those commitments promptly. This shows that you respect their time and take their needs seriously.
- **Maintain professionalism.** While it's important to build rapport, always prioritize their experience over distractions. Be fully present and engaged during every session.

Consistency isn't about perfection; it's about creating a pattern of reliability. Over time, these small, dependable actions build a foundation of trust that encourages clients to stay engaged and open.

## A MOMENT THAT BUILT TRUST

One of my clients walked into her first session back in 2017, and immediately said, "Oh my gosh, I'm such a klutz!", after tripping on the doorframe. A few minutes later, she apologized for being, "the most out-of-shape person in here", and worried aloud about holding others back in the group program she was there to try out for free.

It was clear she was feeling self-conscious and determined to try her hardest, but her energy was running too high—too high for her own safety or the safety of those around her. I had a choice: I could let her push herself in an attempt to prove something, or I could step in to help her find a sustainable starting point.

Rather than calling her out publicly or trying to correct her self-deprecating remarks in the moment, I chose a different path. I acknowledged her concerns with understanding. I recognized that her words weren't just self-criticism—they were an expression of insecurity and fear. Instead of focusing on what she was saying, I listened to what she was really communicating: "I'm nervous. I'm afraid I'll fail."

Quietly and calmly, I approached her when others in the group were occupied, and I reassured her that she was safe. I let her know that the goal of the first session wasn't to keep up with anyone else or to push beyond her limits—it was to find her starting point. Together, throughout that first workout, we focused on building a foundation of movement at a pace and intensity that made her feel capable and confident.

By prioritizing her safety and acknowledging her feelings, I helped her feel at ease. She left that first session knowing she didn't have to compare her journey to anyone else's and, more importantly, that she was in a place where she wouldn't get hurt or be judged. Over time, she not only gained strength but also confidence. She continues to train at my facility to this day, a testament to what can happen when trust and understanding are at the center of coaching.

## PRACTICAL APPLICATIONS

Building trust and rapport isn't just about the first session—it's an ongoing process. These strategies can help you integrate these skills into your coaching while remaining mindful of your client's boundaries:

### *1. Be Intentional*

Begin every session with a simple, open-ended question that invites your client to share how they're feeling. After asking, pause, and give your client the space to respond fully. Listen carefully to their words and tone as well as their body language and facial expressions as these often reveal more than their initial response.

**Key Tip:** Stop talking after you finish asking your question. Listening isn't just about hearing the words—it's about observing their body language, facial expressions, and overall demeanor. More on this in chapter 3.

If your client seems off but chooses not to share, respect their privacy. Avoid probing further and instead demonstrate support through your actions and attention. Clients will open up when they feel ready and trust that you'll listen without judgment.

## 2. Be Flexible

Show clients their input matters by tailoring the session to their needs. For example, if a client mentions feeling fatigued or stressed, be open to adjusting the intensity or focus of the workout to meet them where they are.

**Example:** A client might say, "I didn't sleep well last night, and I feel pretty tired right now."

If you planned a higher-intensity session, you could respond with:

*"Thanks for letting me know. Once we wrap up our mobility and warm-up, let's re-check your energy level and see how you feel then. How does that sound?"*

This approach aligns with the concept of "ooching," as described in *Decisive* by Chip and Dan Heath. Ooching involves taking small, low-risk steps to gather information before making a larger commitment. In this context, starting with lighter mobility work or a warm-up allows you to assess your client's energy and readiness in real-time. If their energy improves, you can gradually increase the session's intensity; if not, you've already built trust by adapting the plan to prioritize their well-being.

By applying ooching in your sessions, you show clients that their feedback matters. This fosters trust and demonstrates your commitment to meeting them where they are, validating their concerns and creating a collaborative dynamic that keeps them engaged and supported.

### 3. Be Smart

Sometimes clients won't feel comfortable sharing personal details, and that's okay. Let them know you're there to listen if they ever need to talk, but don't press for information. Instead, maintain a supportive presence and focus on creating a safe, welcoming training environment.

**Example:** If you notice they seem distracted, you could say:

*"If there's anything on your mind that you'd like to share, I'm here for you. If not, that's perfectly fine too."*

No matter what your client chooses to share with you, remember, you are a fitness professional. Your role as a trainer is to guide clients toward their fitness goals while demonstrating integrity and professionalism. While it's natural to care about your clients and want to support them, it's essential to understand your boundaries. Your personal training certification does not qualify you to act as a counselor, therapist, or psychiatrist.

Be smart. Listen. Offer encouragement. Celebrate their wins and sympathize with their struggles when appropriate. Don't lower your inner integrity. Remember, your job is not to solve their personal challenges or provide advice or solutions to problems outside the scope of fitness. If a client shares something deeply personal, hold their trust with respect and confidence, but resist the urge to step beyond your expertise. The best way to help them in these situations is often to recommend they seek the appropriate professional support. This honors their trust,

# BUILDING TRUST: THE FOUNDATION OF COACHING | 35

protects you, and ensures they receive the care they need. If at any time you feel uncomfortable with what a client is sharing with you, you are not obligated to listen, but you are obligated to communicate that you are not comfortable with it immediately. If you don't stop them from talking, they won't stop talking.

### *4. Be Perceptive*

As a coach, your ability to read non-verbal cues can significantly enhance your connection with clients. Subtle changes in posture, energy levels, or facial expressions often reveal more than words can. By staying attuned to these signals, you can adapt your coaching style in real time to better meet your client's needs.

**What to Watch For:**

- **Posture:** Slouching or tension might signal fatigue, discouragement, or discomfort. Conversely, upright posture and engaged movements often indicate confidence or enthusiasm.
- **Energy Levels:** If a client seems unusually lethargic or overly energetic, it could be a sign of emotional or physical stress that may impact the session.
- **Facial Expressions:** Frowns, hesitation, or blank stares may indicate confusion or self-doubt, while smiles and nods often signal understanding and comfort.

**Building the Habit of Perception:**

- **Slow Down and Observe:** Make it a habit to pause during sessions and observe your client's body language, tone of voice, and overall demeanor.
- **Ask Open-Ended Questions:** If you're unsure about what you're seeing, check-in gently.
  - *"How's this feeling for you so far? Is there anything we should adjust?"*
- **Be Patient:** Remember, not every signal needs immediate action. Sometimes clients just need a moment to reset or process on their own.

By sharpening your ability to notice and respond to your client's signals, you show that you're more than just a coach focused on results—you're a partner who genuinely cares about their journey.

### *5. Be Consistent*

Trust is solidified through the small, reliable actions you take day after day. Your consistency in showing up prepared, keeping your word, and delivering value signals to clients that they can count on you—an essential foundation for a lasting relationship.

**Key Practices:**

- **Show Up Prepared:** Consistency starts with being punctual and ready to engage fully in every session.
- **Follow Through Thoughtfully:** If you promise to provide resources or adjust their program, act promptly and with care. This demonstrates that you value their time and trust.
- **Demonstrate Professionalism:** Maintain a friendly yet professional demeanor, and prioritize their experience over distractions.

**Example:** Imagine a client mentions wanting resources on recovery techniques. Following through promptly with personalized suggestions not only shows reliability but also highlights your attentiveness to their individual needs.

**Insight:** Consistency isn't just about meeting expectations —it's about exceeding them in small but meaningful ways. When clients know you'll deliver on your promises and respect their journey, they feel valued, which strengthens the trust at the heart of the coaching relationship.

## CLOSING THOUGHTS: THE FOUNDATION OF CONNECTION

Every relationship starts with rapport, and over time, rapport matures into trust. As a coach, your role goes beyond simply helping clients move better or achieve their fitness goals. You're creating a space where they feel truly seen, heard, and valued. This extends far beyond the workout itself—it's about fostering an environment where they begin to believe in themselves because they know you believe in them.

It's one thing to believe a client is capable of something you know they can achieve; it's another to help them see that in themselves. Your partnership offers the kind of support and guidance that empowers them to unlock their full potential.

Remember, earning trust takes time, and it requires more than technical skill. Authenticity, empathy, patience, and consistency aren't add-ons to your coaching practice; they are its foundation. These qualities are what set exceptional coaches apart. They remind clients that they are not just a number in your schedule but a valued individual whose growth and success genuinely matter to you.

Trust isn't built through grand gestures—it grows in the quiet moments. It's the warm greeting that makes a client feel welcome, the thoughtful adjustment that prioritizes their needs, and the celebration of their progress, no matter how small. Each of these moments reinforces the bond between you and your client, strengthening your partnership one step at a time.

BUILDING TRUST: THE FOUNDATION OF COACHING | 39

As Stephen Covey reminds us:

> *"Trust is the glue of life. It's the most essential ingredient in effective communication. It's the foundational principle that holds all relationships."*

When you lead with trust, you transform your sessions into something far greater than a series of exercises. You create a relationship where clients feel supported, understood, and inspired to grow. And in doing so, you enrich not only their lives but your own as well. Coaching, at its best, is a mutual journey—one that's as fulfilling for the coach as it is transformative for the client.

So, as you move forward in your career, hold onto this: Every session is an opportunity to strengthen the foundation of trust. Every client is a chance to build a relationship that lasts. And every moment is a reminder of the incredible privilege it is to walk alongside someone as they strive to become the best version of themselves.

### *Coaching Insights: A Quick Recap*

1. **Authenticity:** Be real, honest, and transparent in every interaction. Clients trust coaches who show up as their genuine selves.
2. **Empathy:** Understand your clients' unique stories and meet them where they are—physically, emotionally, and mentally.
3. **Patience:** Respect the client's timeline. Trust is a

journey, not a race, and progress unfolds differently for everyone.
4. **Consistency:** Be reliable in your actions, words, and follow-through. Small, consistent gestures build the foundation for lasting trust.

*Next Steps: Practical Applications*

1. **Practice Observation:** Spend one session focusing solely on observing your client's non-verbal cues. Note their posture, energy, and expressions, and adapt your coaching style accordingly.
2. **Start Each Session Intentionally:** Begin every session with a thoughtful question, such as, "How are you feeling today?" Practice active listening to let them know their response matters.
3. **Celebrate Small Wins:** Identify one small victory in every session—whether it's a movement mastered or a mindset shift—and highlight it to reinforce progress.
4. **Reflect on Your Consistency:** At the end of the week, evaluate your reliability. Did you follow through on promises, show up prepared, and stay engaged?

# 3

# COMMUNICATING EFFECTIVELY

## WHY COMMUNICATION MATTERS

Communication is the lifeblood of coaching. It's not just about what you say—it's about how you say it, how you listen, and how you make your clients feel understood. At its best, communication transforms coaching from a simple exchange of instructions into a meaningful connection. It builds trust, enhances clarity, and motivates clients to push beyond their perceived limits.

But great communication doesn't happen by accident. It requires intentionality and practice. Many trainers focus solely on delivering knowledge or program design, missing the critical step of how that information is received and understood by their clients. Miscommunication, even when unintentional, can create frustration or insecurity. In contrast, effective communication fosters trust and creates an environment where clients feel safe to grow.

Communication is about more than delivering instructions—it's about connecting. It's about being present in the moment and adapting to the person standing in front of you. This is what sets great coaches apart. It's not just what you know, but how you share that knowledge and how you create space for your clients to feel heard, valued, and empowered.

This chapter begins by introducing the four primary methods of communication: verbal, non-verbal, visual, and tactile. Each method serves a unique purpose, and together, they form the foundation of effective communication. By mastering these communication tools, you'll be better equipped to connect with your clients, foster trust building, and create clarity in every session.

Later in this chapter, we'll dive deeper into the art of listening—learning how to interpret your clients' verbal, non-verbal, and visual cues with intentionality. Listening isn't just about hearing; it's about understanding what's being communicated, even when it's unspoken.

Let's jump into the first section:

## PART 1: THE FOUR METHODS OF COMMUNICATION

1. **Verbal Communication:** The words you use and how you deliver them.

2. **Non-Verbal Communication:** Your body language, posture, and facial expressions.
3. **Visual Communication:** Demonstrations, diagrams, and visual aids that reinforce understanding.
4. **Tactile Communication:** Using touch (with consent) to guide movement and help clients feel what they need to focus on.

Each method plays a vital role in creating clarity and connection. While they help your client understand what to do in the moment, they also build rapport that, over time, matures into trust. Together, these methods form a comprehensive communication toolbox, enabling you to meet clients where they are and ensure they feel supported and fully informed.

Let's explore each method in detail.

### *1. Verbal Communication: Beyond Words*

Verbal communication is often the most visible form of interaction between a coach and a client, but it's also one of the most nuanced. It's not just about the words you say—it's about how they are received and understood. Whether you're explaining a movement, offering feedback, or setting expectations, the clarity and intentionality of your words can mean the difference between confusion and confidence. Verbal communication is where trust and understanding begin.

**Clarity and Simplicity**

When giving instructions or feedback, avoid technical jargon or overly complex explanations. Your goal is to deliver information in a way that resonates with your client and drives action. Every client processes information differently, so what works for one may not work for another. Your role is to adapt and find an approach that ensures your client fully understands and feels confident doing what you're telling them.

**Key Points:**

- Speak in terms your client can easily grasp. For example, instead of saying, *"Engage your rectus abdominis,"* you might say, *"Tighten your core like someone's about to poke your stomach."*
- Be concise. Longer explanations can overwhelm clients, so I generally aim for 20-90 second explanations depending on the complexity of the movement or concept.

**Tone Matters: The Energy You Bring**

Your tone doesn't just convey information—it sends a deliberate message to your client. It's not just what you say, but how you say it that sets the emotional tone for the session.

Imagine this: If you were the first person to discover a fire in a building, how would your voice sound? Would you whisper in a high-pitched tone, hoping someone might catch on? Or would you shout with urgency and authority, making it unmistakably clear that evacuation is critical? Think of Godzilla smashing through the streets of Tokyo—there's no ambiguity in the energy or intent of that scenario. The tone of your voice immediately conveys the gravity of the moment.

Now, think about your tone during a training session. Are you signaling to your client that you're engaged, focused, and excited to be there with them? Or does your tone unintentionally suggest boredom, frustration, or disinterest?

**The Message Behind the Energy**

Your tone is the emotional undercurrent of every interaction. Whether you're hyping them up for a big lift, calming their nerves before trying something new, or simply checking in during a warm-up, your tone tells them everything they need to know about your presence and priorities.

**Have You Considered This Before?**

Ask yourself:

- Does my tone reflect the energy I want my clients to feel?
- Am I conveying encouragement, excitement, and belief in their potential?
- Or does my tone unintentionally communicate fatigue, distraction, or hesitation?

## A Practical Reminder

Tone isn't about putting on a show or faking enthusiasm; it's about aligning your energy with the moment. Just as you'd adjust your volume and urgency to warn someone of danger, adjust your tone in training to match your client's needs. Bring intentionality to your sessions: be the coach whose tone says, I'm here, I care, and I believe in you.

## Pace and Delivery

The speed and rhythm of your speech affect how well your clients can process and apply what you're saying. Speaking too quickly can overwhelm, while speaking too slowly can cause disengagement. Aim for a conversational pace that allows time for absorption but keeps the session moving forward.

**Practice Reps:** Record yourself explaining a movement or concept. Review your pace, tone, and clarity. Ask yourself:

- Am I speaking too quickly or too slowly?
- Am I pausing to let the client process what I'm saying?
- Does my tone convey encouragement and professionalism?

## Giving Feedback Thoughtfully

Many trainers believe that giving feedback is simply part of the job, but effective feedback requires a foundation of trust. It's a privilege, not a right, to challenge clients to improve. Before offering constructive criticism, ensure your client trusts that your intentions are rooted in their growth, not in your ego.

Feedback should feel like a partnership, not a critique. Invite clients into the process by asking open-ended questions, such as:

- *"How did that feel?"*
- *"What did you notice about your movement?"*
- *"Is there anything you'd like to adjust?"*

When feedback is delivered with empathy and the intent to collaborate, it becomes an opportunity for growth rather than a point of contention.

### Refining Your Verbal Communication

Effective verbal communication requires continuous self-awareness and practice. Use these prompts to refine your delivery:

- Am I tailoring my language to my client's understanding?
- Am I speaking with clarity and confidence?
- Am I using a tone that motivates and supports?

By taking the time to reflect on and refine your verbal communication, you not only help your clients succeed but also reinforce the trust and rapport that define an exceptional coaching relationship.

## 2. Non-Verbal Communication: What Your Body Says

Clients often express as much through their body language as they do with words. Subtle cues like a slumped posture, diverted eyes, or fidgeting can reveal discomfort, fatigue, or hesitation. Non-verbal communication is about recognizing these signals and responding in ways that make clients feel understood and supported. It's equally about your own body language and what it conveys to your clients.

### Reading Clients' Cues

Learning to interpret your clients' non-verbal signals is a key skill for any coach. These cues can tell you how your client is feeling in the moment and whether they're engaged, discouraged, or distracted.

### Signs to Watch For:

- Slumped posture or averted eyes: These may indicate fatigue, discouragement, or discomfort.
- Fidgeting or crossed arms: This could signal frustration, resistance, or nervousness.
- Tense facial expressions: These might reveal confusion or a lack of confidence in a movement.

### Example:

A client hesitates to attempt a new movement and avoids eye contact. Instead of pushing forward, you might say:

- "Let's take a second to reset. I want to make sure you feel comfortable with this before we move on."

This communicates that you're present with them, reassures them that this is their time, not yours, and builds trust while encouraging their confidence.

**Your Non-Verbal Signals**

Your clients are always observing you. They notice how you stand, your facial expressions, and even where your attention is directed. These non-verbal cues can either enhance your connection with them or unintentionally distance you.

**Key Practices for Coaches:**

- **Maintain Eye Contact:** This conveys that you're engaged and paying attention.
- **Use an Open Posture:** Avoid a closed-off stance or turning away from clients during conversations or demonstrations. Face them, and relax.
- **Minimize Distractions:** Avoid checking your phone or letting your eyes wander during sessions.

**Practical Example:**

If a client is performing reps during a timed sequence, focus on your client rather than staring at the clock. It's ok to glance at the clock every 10 or 15 seconds to get an idea of how much time is left (depending on the length of your set). Keeping your attention on your client ensures you don't miss key information about their form or effort and signals your undivided attention during the session.

**Building Presence**

Being physically present isn't enough. To truly connect, you must project a sense of engagement and positivity. Simple gestures can make a big difference in how valued and supported a client feels.

**Small Gestures That Matter:**

- A fist bump or high five after a challenging set.
- A smile when they've made progress or overcome a struggle.
- A nod of encouragement during moments of hesitation.

These actions don't need to be dramatic, but they should feel authentic. They help create an environment where clients feel appreciated and motivated.

*3. Visual Communication: Show, Don't Just Tell*

Most clients are visual learners. While verbal instructions are essential, pairing them with visual demonstrations can help clarify complex movements or concepts. A demonstration often bridges the gap between understanding and execution.

### Effective Demonstration

When demonstrating exercises, position yourself so the client has an unobstructed view. Focus on clarity and keep demonstrations concise—ideally under 90 seconds, assuming you have more than 1 movement per sequence to demonstrate as well.

### Breaking Down a Movement:

1. Demonstrate the full movement at a controlled pace.
2. Break it into phases, highlighting key actions.
3. It might help to emphasize a common movement fault to help clients avoid them.

### Example: Teaching a Deadlift

- **Step 1:** Demonstrate the entire deadlift movement from start to finish.
- **Step 2:** Break it into three phases: setup, brace, and execute.
- **Step 3:** Use clear language to guide attention: *"Notice how my back stays straight and my weight stays in my heels throughout the movement."*

### Leveraging Visual Aids

Sometimes, even the clearest demonstration isn't enough. Tools like videos, diagrams, or progress charts can provide additional clarity. These aids are especially useful for clients who may struggle to grasp a movement initially.

**Example:**

A client struggling to feel a loss of lumbar stability in a squat or deadlift may benefit from watching a video of their own form. This visual comparison can help them connect the dots, become more aware of their body, and make the necessary adjustments.

**Tailoring Visuals to Clients**

Every client learns differently. While one client might thrive with a live demonstration, another may benefit from diagrams or repetition. Pay attention to how your clients respond and adapt your approach accordingly.

*4. Tactile Communication: Guiding Through Touch*

Tactile communication provides clients with direct feedback through their nervous system. When used appropriately, it can help clients feel the adjustments they need to make in real-time. However, it requires sensitivity and respect for personal boundaries.

**How to Use Tactile Cues**

Tactile communication should always be purposeful and brief. It's about guiding clients, not performing the movement for them.

### Examples of Tactile Cues:

- **Guiding Muscle Focus:** A light tap on the shoulder blades during a row to emphasize contraction in the back.
- **Correcting Balance:** Gently placing hands on the hips to help with alignment during a squat.

### Establishing Boundaries

Always seek consent before using tactile communication. A simple question like, *"Would it be okay if I place my hand here to guide you?"* ensures the client feels respected. Some clients may decline, and that's okay—there are other ways to achieve the same goal.

### When to Use Tactile Communication

This method is especially effective for clients who struggle with proprioception or understanding how a movement should feel. Use tactile cues sparingly and only when they provide value.

### Important Reminder:

Never assume permission based on your role as a coach. Communication and respect are key to maintaining trust in your client relationships.

Also, never try to give a tactile cue when someone is doing an explosive movement like a power clean or a box jump.

## PART 2: LISTENING TO CLIENTS' COMMUNICATION

Communication is a two-way street. While much of this chapter focuses on how you communicate with clients, it's equally vital to understand how your clients communicate with you. Listening—both actively and empathetically—builds trust, clarifies intentions, and ensures that your coaching aligns with your clients' needs and goals.

Listening is not just about hearing the words your clients say; it's about interpreting everything they communicate, from their tone of voice and body language to their willingness to engage. When done well, listening creates a collaborative environment where clients feel truly understood.

### *Encouraging Client Feedback*

Clients can often be hesitant to share discomfort or confusion about a movement. Whether it's due to pride, fear of judgment, or a simple lack of awareness, they might avoid speaking up. So, that means you have to learn how to create an atmosphere where they are invited to engage in the process with you.

Getting your clients to share their thoughts can be as simple as asking the right questions. Open-ended prompts invite clients to reflect and express themselves honestly.

*Active Listening: Beyond Words*

When clients do share their thoughts, your job is to listen with intent and understanding. This means focusing on their words, tone, facial expression, and body language rather than formulating your next response.

**Key Practices for Active Listening:**

- **Pause Before Responding:** Give clients time to finish their thoughts. Avoid interrupting, even if you think you know what they're going to say.
- **Reflect What You Hear:** Paraphrase or repeat their statements to confirm your understanding. For example, *"It sounds like you're feeling some discomfort in your shoulders during that movement. Is that right?"*
- **Validate Their Perspective:** Acknowledge their experience without judgment. Even if you don't agree, phrases like, *"I can see why you'd feel that way"*, demonstrate respect.

*Building a Collaborative Feedback Loop*

Feedback is most effective when it's a two-way conversation. By inviting your clients into the process, you empower them to take ownership of their growth.

**Steps to Create a Feedback Loop:**

1. **Ask for Input:** Begin each session by asking how they're feeling or if there's anything they want to focus on.
2. **Listen Actively:** Give them space to share without interrupting.
3. **Validate and Adjust:** Show you value their input by making adjustments based on their feedback.

**Example:**

If a client says, *"I feel like my lower back is doing too much during deadlifts,"*

Respond with: *"Thanks for letting me know. Let's adjust your form and focus on engaging your glutes and core more."*

Then really watch their technique and make sure you're not missing something. After their next set, check in with them immediately to see and hear what they are communicating. Did the discomfort go away? If so, awesome! If not, do you know why? If not, it's best to not push through. It's best for the client to live to lift another day, and for you to seek some guidance on what could be going wrong for your client in their movement pattern.

*Adapting Your Approach*

Not every client communicates the same way. Some are naturally open, while others may need time to establish some rapport with you. As their coach, your ability to adapt to their unique communication style is crucial.

**Practical Steps for Adaptation:**

- Observe how they respond to your questions and feedback. Are they hesitant or eager to engage?
- Tailor your communication style to match their preferences. For example, some clients thrive on encouragement, while others prefer direct, constructive feedback.
- Continuously assess and adjust. If one approach isn't working, don't be afraid to try something new.

*Practical Techniques to Sharpen Your Listening Skills*

Effective listening is a skill that can—and should—be practiced regularly. Here are some exercises to help you refine this critical component of coaching:

1. **Video Review:**

Record part of a session with your client (with their consent). Watch it back and focus on your listening habits.

- Are you giving your client enough time to speak?
- Are you responding thoughtfully, or are you rushing to reply?
- Are you missing any non-verbal cues?

2. **Role Reversal:**

Have a colleague or friend play the role of the client while you practice listening and responding. Focus on validating their input and adapting your feedback based on what they share.

3. **Client Surveys:**

Ask your clients for feedback on how you listen and communicate during sessions. Questions like, "Do you feel heard during our sessions?" or "What could I do to make communication easier for you?" can provide valuable insights. Surveys are a powerful way to show clients that you value their input and are committed to improving their experience.

To gain an even deeper understanding of your strengths and weaknesses, consider selecting a few trusted clients for more in-depth feedback. Choose individuals with professional experience in customer service or leadership roles and who you know can offer candid, constructive insights. These clients should also be mature enough to provide honest feedback without fear of jeopardizing the professional relationship. With their permission, interview them about their overall experience—covering first impressions, session delivery, and communication style. Ask questions like:

- "What was your first impression of my coaching approach?"

- "Are there ways I can improve how I guide or motivate you during sessions?"
- Is there anything I could do differently to enhance your overall experience?"

This approach not only uncovers blind spots but also allows you to see your coaching through their eyes. By understanding their perspectives, you gain invaluable insights into how your methods align—or don't align—with their needs and expectations.

By combining intentional listening with effective verbal and non-verbal communication, and by leveraging the insights from client feedback, you create a coaching environment where clients feel truly understood. This not only improves their performance but also deepens the trust and rapport that make your coaching relationships thrive.

*Sharpening Your Communication Skills*

Becoming a great communicator doesn't happen overnight—it's a process of consistent reflection and practice. By honing your ability to convey ideas clearly, listen deeply, and adapt to each client, you create an environment that fosters trust, engagement, and growth.

This section offers practical exercises and actionable steps to sharpen your verbal, non-verbal, visual, and tactile communication. These tools will not only improve your effectiveness as a coach but also deepen your connection with your clients.

### 1. Record Yourself Speaking

One of the simplest and most revealing exercises is recording yourself during a session. This allows you to assess your tone, pace, and clarity of speech.

**Action Steps:**

1. Choose a movement or concept to explain and record yourself delivering the explanation.
2. Review the recording and evaluate:
   - Is your tone supportive and engaging?
   - Are you speaking too quickly or too slowly?
   - Are you giving clients enough time to process the information?

**Bonus Challenge:**

Share your recording with a colleague or friend and ask for their honest feedback. Were they able to understand and apply what you explained? Use their input to refine your next delivery.

### 2. Non-Verbal Reflection

Clients read your body language just as much as they listen to your words. Reviewing your non-verbal communication can help you identify areas for improvement.

**Action Steps:**

1. Record a session (with your client's consent) and focus on your posture, gestures, and facial expressions.
2. Reflect on the following:
    - Are you maintaining eye contact and open posture?
    - Are your gestures supportive and intentional, or do they distract from your message?
    - Does your body language convey confidence and presence?

**Ask Yourself:**

If you were the client in this session, would you feel engaged and valued? If not, what could you adjust to improve?

### 3. Practice Tactile Communication

Tactile cues, when used appropriately, can be powerful tools for guiding movement and building body awareness. However, they require a high level of trust and consent.

**Action Steps:**

1. Identify a movement where tactile feedback would be beneficial (e.g., guiding shoulder blade retraction during a row).
2. With the client's consent, provide a gentle, specific tactile cue and observe their response.

3. Reflect on the experience:
   - Did the client understand the correction?
   - Did the cue enhance their movement or create discomfort?

**Reminder:**

Always ask for permission before using tactile communication. A simple question like, "Would it be okay if I guide your shoulder placement?" demonstrates respect and professionalism.

### 4. Survey Your Clients

The best way to improve your communication is to ask for feedback from the people who experience it firsthand—your clients.

**Action Steps:**

1. Create a brief, anonymous survey with questions like:
   - *"Do you feel heard during our sessions?"*
   - *"Are my instructions clear and easy to follow?"*
   - *"What could I do to improve our communication?"*
2. Review the responses with an open mind and identify recurring themes or suggestions.
3. Make specific changes based on the feedback and follow up with your clients to show you value their input.

**Pro Tip:**

Thank clients for their honesty, even if the feedback is challenging to hear. Their insights are invaluable for your growth.

### 5. Role Reversal Practice

Working with a peer or mentor to simulate a client-coach interaction can provide new perspectives on your communication style.

**Action Steps:**

1. Partner with a colleague or friend and switch roles—they act as the coach while you play the client.
2. After the session, discuss:
    - How did their communication style make you feel?
    - Were their instructions clear and supportive?
    - What lessons can you apply to your own coaching?

### 6. Develop a Feedback Ritual

Establishing a routine for giving and receiving feedback can enhance communication in every session.

**Action Steps:**

1. Begin each session by asking, *"Is there anything you'd like to focus on or adjust today?"*
2. Conclude with a reflection question, such as:
   - *"What felt great today?"*
   - *"What could we work on more next time?"*
3. Use these moments to create a feedback loop that strengthens your connection with the client.

**Consistency Is Key**

The exercises above are not one-time tasks—they're habits to be cultivated throughout your coaching career. The more intentional you are about practicing and refining your communication, the more natural and effective it will become.

*Final Reminder*

Communication is not just a skill; it's an ongoing practice that evolves with experience. By dedicating time to reflection and improvement, you demonstrate your commitment to excellence—not only for your clients but also for yourself. Remember, every small adjustment you make brings you closer to becoming the coach your clients deserve.

## *Closing Thoughts*

My dad used to say, "Communication is more than just your words." He was right. Communication isn't just about speaking—it's about connecting. It's about truly reaching the person you're speaking with and letting them reach you in return.

Every word you choose, every gesture you make, and every moment you listen sends a message. But the most profound form of communication is not what you say—it's how you make your clients feel. When you truly listen, when you pay attention to the subtle cues in their body language and tone, you create a space where they feel safe, valued, and understood.

This chapter has explored the many layers of communication: verbal, non-verbal, visual, and tactile. Each of these methods plays a crucial role in building trust and deepening the coach-client connection. But the most transformative element of communication lies in its authenticity. Clients aren't looking for perfection; they're looking for someone who genuinely cares.

As you reflect on this chapter and put these strategies into practice, remember: communication isn't about proving how much you know—it's about showing how much you care. It's about creating a partnership where clients feel empowered to grow, knowing they have your full support.

Every session is an opportunity to strengthen the foundation of trust. Every interaction is a chance to deepen the connection. And every client is a reminder of the privilege it is to guide someone on their journey toward becoming their best self.

So, as you move forward, keep this in mind:

- Be intentional with your words.
- Be present with your actions.
- Be humble in your approach.

Because when communication becomes more than words —when it becomes connection—that's when coaching transcends the gym floor and transforms lives.

# 4

## THE COACH'S MINDSET

Coaching is more than delivering workouts. At its heart, coaching is about building relationships that inspire and empower your clients to grow—not just in their fitness journey, but in their confidence and character.

The best coaches aren't defined by their knowledge alone—they're defined by their intention. They show up with self-awareness, empathy, and adaptability creating an environment where clients feel seen, valued, and motivated to succeed. At the foundation of effective coaching lies your mindset. It's about the energy and focus you bring to each session and the way you show up for your clients—ready to guide them, support them, and lead them toward their goals.

## WHAT IS A COACHING MINDSET?

The coaching mindset is the foundation that shapes every interaction you have with your clients. It's not just about knowledge or skills—it's about the perspective and qualities you bring to your role. This mindset allows you to see beyond the mechanics of a workout and understand the deeper needs of the person in front of you.

At its core, a coaching mindset is about growth—both for you and your clients. It requires humility to acknowledge where you can improve, empathy to connect with your clients' unique challenges, and leadership to guide them toward their goals with confidence and care.

This mindset isn't static; it's something you cultivate through intentional reflection and consistent effort. When you commit to showing up with purpose, your sessions transform from a series of exercises into meaningful opportunities for connection, progress, and trust.

By embracing a coaching mindset, you can create an environment where your clients feel safe to grow—and where you, as their coach, can grow alongside them.

### *A Growth-Oriented Mindset*

Coaching begins with a belief in the potential for growth—not just for your clients, but for yourself. Growth isn't linear or easy; it's a process of embracing setbacks as opportunities to learn, adapt, and refine as you go. A growth-oriented mindset means seeing challenges not as obstacles, but as necessary steps along the journey to improvement.

The first year in this profession is often the most challenging. The steep learning curve, the demands of the role, and the weight of responsibility can overwhelm even the most passionate trainers. Many leave the industry before they've had a chance to fully develop their potential. But those who adopt a growth-oriented mindset find a way through. They approach each day as an opportunity to learn, seek mentorship from those who've walked the path before them, and remain resilient in the face of setbacks.

Oftentimes, we are our own worst critic. Growth takes persistence and this mindset requires a commitment to your own evolution as a coach. Just as you guide your clients toward their goals, this mindset will guide you toward yours, turning the early struggles of your career into the foundation for a long and fulfilling journey.

## EMPATHY-DRIVEN COACHING

Empathy is at the heart of a strong coaching mindset. It's the ability to see beyond the surface and take the time to understand your clients' unique stories—their goals, fears, challenges, and victories. Empathy is what turns coaching from a transactional exchange into transformational experience.

True empathy requires presence. To truly connect with your clients, you must leave distractions and assumptions behind and focus entirely on their needs in the moment. When you listen with empathy, you give your clients the space to express their challenges without rushing to fix them. Instead, you reflect on their words, paraphrase to confirm understanding, and validate their feelings. That's active listening in a nutshell. This doesn't mean you need to have all the answers—it means you need to be fully present, showing your clients that you're invested in their growth.

Presence isn't just about listening—as stated in the previous chapter—it's about observing body language, noticing shifts in tone or mood, and responding thoughtfully and intentionally. It's about making your client feel like they are the most important person in the room.

When you coach with this level of empathy, you help clients experience your support which in turn will empower them to move forward, even when doubts or setbacks arise. Remember, you're not just guiding them toward their goals; you're showing them that their journey, struggles, and triumphs all matter.

## LEADERSHIP-FOCUSED COACHING

John C. Maxwell said in *The 21 Irrefutable Laws of Leadership* (1998):

> *"Leadership is influence—nothing more, nothing less."*

Influence doesn't happen overnight. Being a certified personal trainer doesn't make you any more of a leader than driving a car makes you a race car driver. Leadership grows through consistent care, patient understanding, and unwavering support. Consistency is key. Show up with integrity and deliver your best effort, session after session. As a coach, leadership is about finding the balance between authority and approachability. Your clients need you to guide them with clarity and compassion, showing confidence in their ability to succeed while remaining adaptable to their needs.

Too often, young trainers get fixated on immediate outcomes—like seeing dramatic client transformations—and miss the chance to build deeper trust by investing time in truly understanding their clients. Leadership isn't about rushing toward results; it's about focusing on the process and building a foundation of trust with your client.

True leadership is about inspiring belief—not just in the program, but in the client themself. At Precision Training, our coaching culture prioritizes building genuine relationships with each of our clients. Coaching, to us, is about truly connecting with individuals—understanding their unique goals, challenges, and motivations—while fostering an environment rooted in trust and collaboration.

When you approach each session with this kind of care and intention, you give your clients something far more valuable than a workout: you show them that they're capable of growth and success.

## WHY MINDSET MATTERS

Think about a mentor or teacher who made a lasting impact on your life. Chances are, it wasn't just their knowledge that stood out—it was the way they made you feel. Maybe they believed in you when you didn't believe in yourself, or they guided you through challenges with patience and encouragement.

Isn't that the kind of coach you want to be?

At the heart of a coaching mindset is empowering your clients to take ownership of their journey. When clients feel powerless—whether it's over their schedule, their habits, or their ability to succeed—it's your job to remind them of their agency. This belief isn't just about motivation; it's about creating a shift in perspective. It helps clients reframe even their struggles as meaningful steps on their journey to success. The coaching mindset allows you to lead with purpose, connect with clients on a deeper level, and inspire real lasting change.

Fostering this mindset isn't always easy. It requires both coaches and clients to step outside their comfort zones. For you, it means embracing discomfort in your own growth—adapting when sessions don't go as planned, learning from mistakes, and staying patient with the process. For your clients, it means trusting that even small, consistent changes can lead to a new version of themselves.

You can't always control the circumstances of a session—whether a client feels motivated, whether life throws obstacles in their way, or whether progress feels slower than expected. But you can control how you respond. The energy, encouragement, and support you bring to each session set the tone for your client's experience and build the foundation of trust they'll rely on.

The coaching mindset goes beyond workouts and results. It's about fostering an environment where clients feel supported in their growth and progress, no matter the challenges they face. It's about becoming a leader who not only helps clients achieve their goals but equips them with the confidence and tools to continue growing long after your time together.

## BRIDGING THE GAP: FROM MINDSET TO APPROACH

Your mindset as a coach doesn't just shape how you view yourself—it directly influences how you approach every client interaction. A coaching mindset rooted in growth, empathy, and leadership will naturally guide you to prioritize the client's experience.

Early in my career, I learned this lesson the hard way.

One day, my boss pulled me into his office and told me about a potential new client who had scheduled a trial session. She worked at a law office nearby and was considering signing up her entire team for training at our gym. My boss emphasized the stakes: "You have to give her an amazing workout," he said. "Work her hard. She said she didn't have a good experience with her last trainer, so show her why we're different."

I was eager to impress, and when she walked into the gym, I was immediately struck by how fit she looked. Her toned arms and confident demeanor made me assume she was ready for an intense workout. I dove right in, taking her through the plan I'd prepared. I showed her each exercise, demonstrated the proper form, and made sure to count every rep she did. I even offered cues and adjustments to ensure her technique was solid.

We made it through one full round of the workout, and partway into the second, something unexpected happened. In the middle of a set of shoulder presses, she set the weights down, looked me dead in the eye, and said, "Learn how to talk to people." She grabbed her keys and walked out.

I was stunned. Up until that moment, I thought I was doing everything right. I had checked all the boxes: correcting her form, encouraging her, making sure she was braced and breathing properly. But I had completely missed the most important part of coaching: the relationship.

After reflecting on the experience, I realized the problem wasn't my knowledge or the exercises I had chosen—it was my approach. I had treated the session like a task to complete instead of an opportunity to connect. From the moment I shook her hand, I made it all about the workout and not about *her*.

## THE COACHING MINDSET IN ACTION

This experience taught me an invaluable lesson: a task-focused approach will never replace a relationship-centered mindset. A relationship-centered coach prioritizes the client's experience in the moment. Had I approached that session with curiosity and empathy—starting with a simple conversation about her expectations or her past experiences—I could have built trust instead of rushing into the workout. By prioritizing her story over my agenda, I would have shown her that this wasn't just another session—it was her opportunity to feel supported and understood.

Ultimately, this is the heart of a coaching mindset: understanding that the relationship always comes before the reps. By aligning your mindset with your client's experience, you elevate your coaching from functional to transformational. The coaching mindset bridges the gap between what we *know* as trainers and how we *connect* as leaders. It transforms sessions from tasks to relationships, creating an environment where clients can thrive emotionally, mentally, and physically.

Think back to a time when someone truly listened to you versus a time when someone simply told you what to do. Which experience left you feeling more valued, understood, and motivated? Now, ask yourself—are you creating that same feeling of trust with your clients?

When you coach with the client's experience in mind, you show them that their needs, emotions, and progress matter just as much as the workout itself. This doesn't mean the program isn't valuable—it is. The fitness component is the foundation of what we do as trainers, but a great coach uses the program as a flexible tool to meet the client where they are in that moment. By adapting with empathy and intention, you guide them forward at a pace that feels both challenging and supportive.

Ultimately, while the workout is undeniably important, it's the relationship that often keeps clients coming back. The trust and connection you build with your clients elevate their experience and commitment, fostering an environment where they feel seen, valued, and motivated —not just to stay on track with their goals, but to continue choosing you as their coach to help them achieve them.

## SHIFTING FROM "WORKOUT LEADER" TO "COACH"

When trainers focus only on the tasks of a session—delivering the workout, counting reps, and correcting form—they miss the bigger picture. Clients don't just want a workout; they want a connection with someone who sees their potential, understands their challenges, and is genuinely invested in their success.

Take a moment to reflect: When you plan a session, is your first thought, *What exercises do I want to coach today?* If so, consider shifting your perspective. Instead, ask yourself:

- *What does my client need most from me today?*
- *What is the biggest need of my client to truly grow?*

Good coaches don't focus only on what will win a game; they focus on what will make a better athlete. Great coaches take it a step further—they focus on making the individual better. They ask the questions that matter: What is my client's biggest challenge right now? What's holding them back physically, mentally, or emotionally? Sometimes the answer is straightforward—improving a movement pattern, increasing strength, or refining a skill. But often, the client's needs go deeper.

Your client might need encouragement after a tough week, a moment of patience as they work through frustrations, or simply the reassurance that you believe in them—even when they're doubting themselves. By prioritizing the person in front of you over the program in your hand, you show that coaching is about connection, not just correction.

A great coach who prioritizes trust recognizes that clients bring more than just their bodies into a session—they bring their thoughts, feelings, and experiences. The best coaches meet clients where they are, tailoring each interaction to address not only physical needs but emotional and mental states as well.

As a leader, your role isn't just to help your clients achieve their goals—it's to help them feel seen, valued, and supported throughout their journey. This is their story, and you are there to guide, encourage, and empower them along the way. By focusing on the client's biggest needs and prioritizing the relationship over the workout, you create a space where clients feel safe to grow—not just in the gym, but in other areas of their lives as well.

## KEY CHARACTERISTICS OF A STRONG COACHING MINDSET

To develop a mindset that consistently empowers your clients, focus on these three qualities:

### 1. Self-Awareness:

Your mood, energy, and words set the tone for your client's experience. If you're distracted or negative, your client will notice, and it can impact their mindset for the entire session. Self-awareness means being attuned to how your internal state influences the energy you bring to the gym—and taking steps to stay present and focused.

*Practice:* Before each session, ask yourself:

- *Am I bringing the energy and focus my client deserves?*
- *What does my client need most from me today?*

Self-awareness isn't just about recognizing your own emotions—it's about taking intentional action to align your mindset with your role as a coach. By showing up fully engaged, you create an environment where clients can feel your support and, as a result, develop the internal drive to perform at their best.

### *2. Humility: Check Your Ego at the Door*

At its core, humility means setting aside ego to focus on what truly matters—your clients' success. Great coaches don't pretend to know everything. Instead, they build trust by acknowledging what they don't know and committing to finding the best answers. This willingness to prioritize growth over pride demonstrates that your ultimate goal is serving your clients, not maintaining an illusion of expertise.

As Ryan Holiday writes in Ego Is the Enemy:

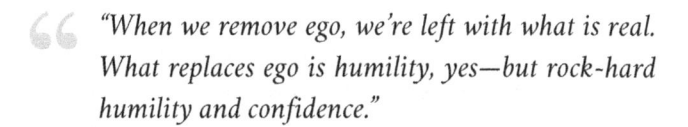

> *"When we remove ego, we're left with what is real. What replaces ego is humility, yes—but rock-hard humility and confidence."*

Humility doesn't mean uncertainty or weakness; it's a confident acknowledgment of the ongoing journey of learning and improvement. It's the realization that there's always room to grow, both as a professional and as a person.

For example, if a client asks about an injury, condition, or topic you're unfamiliar with, humility empowers you to respond like this:

*"That's a great question. I want to make sure I give you the best advice, so let me do some research or consult an expert, and I'll get back to you."*

This approach doesn't diminish your credibility—instead, it enhances it. It shows your clients that their needs come first and that you care enough to find the most accurate, tailored solutions. It also reinforces the idea that coaching is a partnership rooted in trust and respect.

Humility also helps you navigate challenges and setbacks with grace. When you check your ego at the door, you create space for growth. Whether it's learning from a tough session or seeking feedback from a mentor or client, humility keeps you focused on progress rather than perfection. And when your clients see this mindset in action, it inspires them to approach their own journey with the same openness and resilience.

**Key Takeaway:**

Humility is at the core of the coaching mindset. Humility is a virtue we must put into practice. It's about continually choosing to prioritize learning, connection, and service over ego. It's not about us. By cultivating humility, you create stronger relationships with your clients, foster trust, and ensure that your coaching evolves in alignment with your clients' needs.

### 3. Patience and Adaptability: Meeting Clients Where They Are

Humility opens the door for growth, and patience and adaptability are the tools that allow you to walk through it with your clients. Coaching isn't about rigidly sticking to the plan—it's about recognizing that your clients are human, complete with fluctuating energy levels, emotions, and life circumstances. Your ability to respond to their needs with understanding and flexibility is what distinguishes good coaches from truly great ones.

**Patience** means meeting your clients where they are, without judgment or frustration. Remember, progress isn't always linear—setbacks are inevitable, and every session may not go as planned. Your role is to support your clients on both their best and toughest days, creating an environment where they feel safe to show up exactly as they are. When you approach your sessions with patience, you communicate to your clients that their value is not tied to their performance but to their effort and commitment.

**Adaptability** is the art of pivoting when circumstances demand it. While a carefully crafted program is essential, it should serve as a flexible framework, not a rigid script. Clients will have days when they're distracted, stressed, or simply not feeling their best. On those days, sticking to the plan without considering their state can undermine trust and reduce their engagement.

Imagine a client walks in looking visibly stressed and says, *"I'm just not feeling it today."* A task-focused coach might insist on completing the planned workout regardless of their client's emotional state. A relationship-centered coach, however, would adapt the session to better suit the client's needs by saying:

*"No problem. Let's start with some mobility work and see how you feel after that."*

This small adjustment sends a powerful message: *"Your well-being comes first."* It shows that you care about them as a person, not just their ability to complete a workout. Over time, this level of responsiveness builds trust, deepens the coaching relationship, and keeps clients engaged—even on their most challenging days.

PRACTICAL APPLICATION: THE PATIENCE + ADAPTABILITY FORMULA

*Patience + Adaptability = Trust and Long-Term Success*

Patience and adaptability aren't just soft skills—they're the foundation of trust and the key to winning the long game with your clients. Together, they communicate to your clients that you see them as more than just their physical performance. You're acknowledging their humanity while guiding them toward their goals.

Here's how patience and adaptability come together in practice:

1. **Observe and Listen:** Take the time to notice your client's energy, mood, and body language at the start of each session. This creates space for an honest conversation about how they're feeling and what they need.
2. **Acknowledge Their Experience:** Validate their feelings, whether they're tired, stressed, or simply having an off day. A simple acknowledgment can help them feel supported and understood.
3. **Adjust Intentionally:** Modify the session to align with their current state. If they're low on energy, focus on mobility, stretching, or lighter work. If they're feeling strong, lean into the momentum and push a bit harder.

*Patience and Adaptability = Trust*

When clients see that you're not rigidly following a plan but are instead adjusting to meet them where they are, they feel seen and understood. Trust is the outcome, and trust is what keeps clients coming back—even when progress feels slow or life throws challenges their way.

*Patience and Adaptability = Resilience*

By modeling patience and flexibility, you're also teaching your clients a powerful lesson: progress doesn't require perfection. Adaptability fosters resilience, showing them that setbacks are just detours—not dead ends—on the path to success.

Ultimately, **Patience + Adaptability = Long-Term Success.** Clients who trust you and feel supported are more likely to stay consistent, overcome challenges, and develop the confidence to stick with their fitness journey for the long haul.

### *Reflection and Growth*

Coaching is a journey, not a destination. The best coaches aren't those who avoid mistakes but those who commit to learning from them. Reflection is the tool that turns experience into progress, helping you refine your approach and grow into the coach you aspire to be.

At the end of every session—or even every week—take time to reflect on both your successes and your opportunities for growth. Move beyond simple self-assessment and focus on practical steps that will help you improve:

- *What did I do well today, and how can I build on that success in future sessions?*
- *What could I have done better, and what tangible action will I take to improve?*
- *How did my client respond to my coaching today, both verbally and non-verbally? What adjustments might improve their experience next time?*
- *Did I adapt my communication or approach effectively based on my client's needs?*

These questions aren't about nitpicking or perfectionism —they're about fostering intentional growth. By connecting reflection to specific actions, you transform learning into progress, step by step. Just like working out, it's a gradual process of refinement, one session, one interaction at a time. The coaches who stand out are the ones who embrace this process, cultivating the self-awareness and intentionality that set great coaches apart. When you commit to reflection and growth, you're not just building a better career—you'll create a lasting impact in your clients' lives.

*Progress Through Intentionality*

Growth requires more than just time—it requires intention. Simply logging sessions won't lead to transformation; it's the consistent, purposeful effort you put into improving your craft that drives lasting progress.

Intentionality means taking ownership of your development. It's about approaching each session, reflection, and challenge with a mindset focused on learning and refining. Whether you're honing your communication skills, rethinking a client's program, or adjusting based on feedback, each action builds on the last, creating momentum that elevates your coaching over time.

This process is not just for your clients—it's for you. Every deliberate step you take contributes to your growth as a professional and the positive impact you have on the people you serve.

*Chapter Summary: Coaching with Intention*

Your mindset as a coach is the compass that guides every interaction, every decision, and every session. By embracing humility, patience, adaptability, and empathy, you build a foundation that transcends the mechanics of training and creates space for transformation.

Your role as a coach is not just about delivering results; it's about inspiring belief. When your clients feel valued, seen, and supported, they're not just motivated to keep going—they're empowered to believe in their own potential. The relationships you foster through intentional coaching can go beyond the gym.

It's easy to focus on programs, metrics, and goals, but the real impact of your work lies in how you make your clients feel. Coaching is about showing up with purpose, meeting clients where they are, and guiding them with compassion and care. When you prioritize the relationship over the workout, you don't just create progress—you create trust, resilience, and growth that endures far beyond your time together.

# 5

# THE CLIENT JOURNEY

## EVERY CLIENT IS A STORY

Every client who walks through your doors carries a story—a unique set of experiences, fears, goals, and dreams. Some arrive with excitement and clear objectives, while others are hesitant, uncertain about their ability to succeed or even about trusting another trainer. Your role as their coach isn't just to create workout plans or count reps; it's to help them navigate their story and guide them toward a better version of themselves. The client journey is deeply personal, yet universal in its challenges.

To be an effective coach, you must step into their world, meet them where they are, and walk alongside them through every victory and setback. It's a process that requires empathy, adaptability, and an unwavering commitment—not just to their physical goals but to their growth as individuals.

**Key Insight:** Coaching is about connection. A client's success starts with your ability to truly understand their unique journey.

## MEETING CLIENTS WHERE THEY ARE

No two clients start from the same place. Some arrive motivated, with a history of fitness success, ready to jump right into the action. Others walk in uncertain of what they want, what they're capable of, or even whether they belong in the gym at all. Your ability to meet clients where they are is one of the most critical skills you can develop as a coach.

Early in my career, I worked with a client who walked into her first session looking apprehensive. She immediately apologized, saying, "I'm probably going to be your worst client. I'm so out of shape." That comment wasn't just about her fitness level; it revealed a deeper struggle—one that had defined her relationship with exercise for most of her life. She was self-conscious about her appearance and her weight, and for years, she had opted to eat instead of handling her stress in healthier ways. She had tried to start her fitness journey on her own countless times but would always give up within a month. This time, she decided she needed help. She wasn't just looking for a trainer—she was looking for someone who could help her break through the frustration of giving up on herself.

After we finished her assessment, we sat down in my boss's office to go over her results. As I went line by line through the data, I noticed tears filling her eyes. I could see it: the embarrassment, the frustration, the feeling of disappointment that she couldn't hide. But more than that, I could tell she was reading me—waiting to see whether I would judge her or whether I would meet her with understanding.

In that moment, my role as her coach became clear. I adjusted my tone of voice, softened my body language, and kept steady, reassuring eye contact. I wanted her to know, without a doubt, that I wasn't judging her and that she had nothing to feel ashamed of. I paused and said, "Who you are today is not who you're going to be tomorrow. And who you are tomorrow will not stay the same either. One thing I can promise you is that you are going to earn the results that you achieve. As long as we keep open and honest communication, there's nothing that will stop you from being successful."

That conversation was a turning point—not just for her, but for me as a coach. She didn't need someone to throw exercises at her or push her past her limits. She needed someone to believe in her, to help her see herself as capable and strong when she couldn't yet see it for herself.

We started small, focusing on movements that built her confidence. Every bit of progress was celebrated along the way. In her first six months, she lost over 30 pounds, and I'll never forget the moment she showed me a flex picture of her abs—something she never imagined was possible. She planned to train for six months, but she stayed for two years. By the time we finished working together, she was no longer the hesitant, self-doubting person who had walked into the gym that first day. She had become someone who worked out four to six days a week on her own, still in phenomenal shape and proud of the strength she had earned.

Her transformation wasn't just physical—it was mental and emotional. It reminded me that success begins with listening. When you truly hear your client's story, you can build trust and tailor your approach to their unique needs. For her, the most important progress wasn't measured on the scale or in a set of assessments—it was measured in her belief that she was capable of change, and that this time, she wouldn't give up on herself.

### *Practical Application: Meeting Clients Where They Are*

Meeting clients where they are isn't just about adjusting physical programming—it's about understanding their unique preferences, motivations, and boundaries. As a trainer, your role is to guide them toward their goals, not to impose your own ideals or preferences. Your job is to co-create a training experience that resonates with them and keeps them engaged for the long haul.

Consider this: Training is deeply personal. What works for one person might feel restrictive, unenjoyable, or even demotivating for someone else. Encouraging a client to "train their legs more" or "do squats because they're the gold standard" without understanding their preferences might alienate them rather than inspire progress. Instead, focus on fostering a love for movement by making their journey about them.

Here are some practical strategies to meet clients where they are:

1. **Embrace Individuality**

Not everyone wants—or needs—to follow the same path. Some clients might prefer machine-based exercises over free weights, or steady-state cardio over HIIT. That's okay. Training should be an experience that feels rewarding, not a chore. If your client thrives on leg extensions but doesn't enjoy barbell squats, celebrate the effort they're putting in and program accordingly. The key is to help clients find joy in movement so they can stay consistent over time.

Now, think about your own training preferences: What exercises or movements do you genuinely enjoy? How often do you include them in your routine? Imagine if your training program lacked those elements—how would that impact your motivation and consistency? The same applies to your clients. When we create space for their preferences, we help them build a relationship with fitness that lasts.

2. **Focus on Process Over Perfection**

Sustainability beats intensity in the long run. It's better for a client to enjoy their routine and show up regularly than to feel pressured into an "optimal" program they dread. As their trainer, your role is to help them develop a positive relationship with training that prioritizes their well-being—mentally and physically. Goals like a six-pack or peak performance mean nothing if they make the client feel miserable or disconnected from the process.

**Key Mindset:** Training isn't just about outcomes; it's about creating a lifestyle they look forward to.

### 3. Adapt to Their Starting Point

If a client is new to training, start with foundational exercises that build confidence and competence. If they're experienced but struggling with motivation, focus on small wins to rekindle their passion. And if they're dealing with setbacks, such as injuries or life stress, remind them that their training doesn't have to be "all or nothing." Meeting clients where they are means honoring their current circumstances while helping them move forward—at their pace.

**Remember:** Validate their starting point and celebrate progress, no matter how small.

### 4. Ask and Listen

The most effective way to understand your client's needs is to ask open-ended questions and truly listen to their answers. Find out what they want to get out of training, what barriers they're facing, and what success looks like to them. Reflecting their answers back to them not only builds trust but also ensures you're aligned with their vision for their fitness journey.

**Sample Questions:**

- What's one thing you'd love to feel more confident about in your training?
- What kind of workouts have you enjoyed in the past?
- How do you want to feel when you leave a session?

5. **Make It About Their Lifestyle**

Not every client aspires to be a competitive athlete, a bodybuilder, or a fitness model—and that's okay. If your client's goal is to improve their energy levels for work or feel strong enough to play with their kids, those goals are just as valid as a six-pack or increased bench press numbers. Frame their training in a way that aligns with their lifestyle and values.

**Remember:** Fitness isn't a one-size-fits-all formula. It's about creating a path that feels meaningful and sustainable for each client.

By adopting these strategies, you can shift the focus from what you think a client should be doing to what they truly want to do. When training feels enjoyable, personal, and tailored to their unique goals, clients show up—and they keep showing up. That's how you meet them where they are and empower them to move forward.

## GUIDING CLIENTS THROUGH THE HIGHS AND LOWS

Clients will face plateaus, setbacks, and moments of doubt. As a coach, these moments are opportunities to show them that setbacks aren't failures—they're part of the process.

One of my longest-standing clients started training with me after leaving another gym where she'd had a poor experience with an unprofessional trainer. She was hesitant to trust again, and it took months of consistency and patience to rebuild her confidence. There were days when she struggled and wanted to give up, but each time, I reminded her of how far she'd come—not just in terms of physical progress, but in the way she carried herself with more confidence and pride.

Setbacks—be they physical, psychological, or circumstantial—test both the coach and the client. They demand a coach who is adaptable and capable of meeting clients where they are—both emotionally and physically. When unprepared to guide clients through these valleys, coaches risk unintentionally provoking frustration and losing trust. Even worse, this inability to provide perspective and resilience when it matters most almost guarantees failure.

A coach's mindset is one of adaptability, tuned to the varying physical and emotional states of their clients. It's about knowing when to push, when to listen, and when to adjust, ensuring clients feel supported rather than overwhelmed. When you can guide clients through the highs and lows with empathy and intentionality, you turn challenges into milestones, helping them see that progress isn't defined by perfection but by persistence.

**Key Insight:** The way you respond to a client's challenges can determine whether they push through or give up.

For my client, her previous gym experience left her feeling like a failure whenever she didn't set a personal record during workouts. The uphill mental battle she had to overcome was recognizing that progress is rarely immediate but always gradual.

As her coach, my role wasn't just to guide her physically but to shift her mindset. Together, we focused on celebrating small wins, redefining what success looked like, and embracing the process as more than a destination. Over time, she learned to approach her training with a new sense of resilience—one that carried her through the inevitable ups and downs of her journey. Also, the confidence she gained in training extended far beyond the gym, showing her that persistence could overcome doubt in all areas of her life.

*Practical Application: Navigating Highs and Lows*

1. **Ask Solution-Focused Questions**

Instead of focusing on the struggle, guide the client toward actionable steps:

- *"What feels like the hardest part of this for you today?"*
- *"What's one adjustment we can make to keep moving forward?"*

## 2. Highlight Progress in the Moment

Remind clients of how far they've come:

- *"You've improved so much since we started—remember when this was a struggle?"*
- *"Look at how consistent you've been, when was the last time you could say you've worked out this consistently before?"*

## 3. Reframe Tough Days as Wins

Help clients see the value in showing up, even when it's hard:

- *"The fact that you're here today speaks volumes—progress happens on days like this."*
- *"It's okay if today feels tough; that's where growth happens."*

## 4. Set Small, Achievable Goals

Break down challenges into manageable steps to help build confidence:

- *"Let's focus on just one rep at a time and go from there."*

- *"How about we aim for one small win today? What feels achievable?"*

5. **End on a Positive Note**

Leave clients with encouragement that reinforces their efforts:

- *"You showed a lot of grit today. That's the kind of mindset that leads to big results."*
- *"I'm proud of how you handled today's session—this is what progress looks like."*

## MILESTONES AND MEANINGFUL GOALS

Clients often come in with surface-level goals: losing weight, building muscle, or getting stronger. While these are important, they're rarely the whole story. Your job is to help clients uncover the "why" behind their goals—the deeper motivations that drive them.

One client came to me determined to lose 20 pounds. As we talked, it became clear that her goal wasn't about the number—it was about feeling confident enough to join her family on the beach in a bathing suit. By connecting her goal to this meaningful vision, we shifted her focus away from fearing the scale and toward building a strong, fit, and healthy body. That deeper connection kept her motivated, even when the journey felt tough. The best part was that she reached her goal weight and she acquired the confidence to go to the beach with her family in a bathing suit.

**Key Insight:** Goals tied to deeper values inspire lasting commitment. When a goal reflects what truly matters to a client—whether it's confidence, connection, or quality of life—it becomes a powerful source of intrinsic motivation.

*Practical Application: Connecting Goals to Values*

1. **Ask Values-Driven Questions:**

During goal-setting conversations, go beyond surface-level objectives with questions like:

- *"Why is this goal important to you?"*
- *"What will achieving this allow you to do that you can't do now?"*
- *"Who in your life would be most impacted by your success?"*

2. **Reframe the Journey:**

Help clients see how their workouts connect to their broader values. For example:

- Instead of saying, *"This will help you lose weight,"* say, *"This is building the strength and energy you'll need for the life you want."*

- Instead of focusing on the immediate challenge, emphasize how their effort today will pay off tomorrow.

3. **Celebrate Wins That Align With Values:**

Acknowledge milestones that align with their deeper purpose. For example:

- Completing a challenging hike isn't just about physical fitness—it's about proving to themselves that they're capable of more than they imagined.
- Running a 5K isn't just an athletic achievement— it's about honoring their commitment to prioritize health and inspire their family.

4. **Reconnect During Setbacks:**

When motivation dips, remind clients of their *"why"*. Ask reflective questions like:

- *"How will it feel to overcome this challenge?"*
- *"What's one small step we can take today to move closer to your bigger goal?"*

By anchoring goals in their deeper values, you turn the journey into something much more than physical effort— it becomes a pathway to self-discovery and lasting transformation.

## ADAPTING TO THE UNEXPECTED

Life doesn't always go as planned, and neither do training programs. Injuries, stress, and unexpected life events will inevitably arise. Great coaches are the ones who adapt without making clients feel like they're failing.

I remember a client who came to a session after a particularly stressful week and admitted she didn't feel up to her usual workout. Instead of pushing her through the planned session, we shifted focus to mobility, core, and some breathing exercises. By the end of the session, she felt more relaxed and ready to take on the rest of the week.

**Key Insight:** Flexibility is a strength, not a compromise. It's not about lowering standards—it's about meeting clients where they are and keeping them moving forward. The ability to adapt shows clients that you prioritize their well-being, even when the original plan doesn't align with the client's state that day.

### *Empowering Potential*

The ultimate goal of coaching isn't just short-term results—it's creating lasting change. The lessons your clients learn from you should extend beyond the gym, empowering them to live healthier, more fulfilling lives.

One client, who trained with me for years, sent me a photo of herself completing a hike she'd once thought impossible. She told me, *"This never would have happened without you believing in me when I didn't believe in myself."* That's the legacy of coaching—helping people achieve not just their goals but their potential.

**Key Insight:** Coaching transcends fitness—it's about equipping clients with the skills, habits, and mindsets that enable them to thrive in every aspect of life.

*Key Takeaways:*

- Coaching is about partnership, not prescription.
- Meaningful goals tied to deeper values inspire lasting commitment.
- Flexibility and empathy build trust and resilience through challenges.
- Adaptability is essential for navigating setbacks and maintaining trust and helping clients discover their potential.

***Closing Thoughts: Beyond the Gym***

Every session is more than a workout—it's an opportunity to shape a client's story. While sets and reps are the foundation, the true magic happens when you connect with the person behind the goals. It's in the moments when you meet them where they are, guide them through their doubts, and celebrate their victories—no matter how small—that transformation takes root.

When you coach with intention, empathy, and adaptability, you help your clients discover the strength they didn't know they had. It's not just about improving their physical capabilities; it's about unlocking their potential, building their confidence, and inspiring a mindset that empowers them to take on challenges in every area of life.

The impact of your coaching reaches far beyond the gym walls. It's seen in the parent who now has the energy to play with their kids, the professional who walks into a meeting with renewed confidence, or the individual who finally feels at home in their own body. This is the legacy of great coaching: creating a ripple effect that transforms not only workouts, but lives.

Every session is an opportunity—not just to guide a client physically, but to change how they see themselves and what they believe they're capable of. When you focus on the whole person, the journey you create together becomes more than a fitness plan—it becomes a path to lasting growth, self-belief, and fulfillment

## 6

## SHOWING UP FOR YOURSELF AS A COACH

In the fitness industry, the focus is almost always on the client: their progress, their goals, and their challenges. But what happens when the coach is the one struggling? How do you keep showing up when the demands of the profession weigh heavily on your shoulders? Coaching isn't just about being present for the good days—it's about navigating the hard ones, too. And often, the hardest days aren't your clients'; they're your own.

Trainers face a unique dynamic: their success depends on their ability to align their schedules with their clients' lives, often sacrificing their own work-life balance. It's a profession where long hours, inconsistent income, and emotional fatigue are normalized. Many trainers work multiple jobs to make ends meet, juggling commitments across multiple gyms while trying to maintain their health and fitness. For others, the pressure comes from sales quotas or the need to prove themselves in an overcrowded industry. This relentless push to perform takes a toll, leading many talented individuals to burnout or leave the profession altogether.

## FACING BURNOUT AND REDISCOVERING PURPOSE

When I first started at Lifetime Fitness, I had no idea what I was walking into. I thought being a trainer meant mastering program design, exercise science, and anatomy. What I didn't expect was to be handed a $3,000 monthly sales goal in my first month. That meant I had to sell 47 sessions at $65 each. By my third month, I exceeded expectations, hitting a $10,000 revenue milestone. But instead of celebrating, I was told my next month's goal was $12,000. The higher I climbed, the higher the expectations became. One month, I failed to meet my goal, earning $9,000 instead of $12,000, and I felt like a complete failure. I even remember my boss calling me out in front of the whole team for not making my goal. "Don't sandbag next month, Wade". I never forgot that.

I'd pour everything I had into my work, but no matter how much I achieved, it was never enough. The pressure wasn't just external—it was self-inflicted. I wanted to be perfect. I wanted to prove I could do it all. But the more I pushed myself to perform seamlessly, the more I set myself up for burnout. It wasn't until I hit that breaking point that I realized I wasn't just guiding clients through their journeys—I was on a journey of my own.

*Facing Burnout at a Private Gym*

When I moved into the private gym setting, I thought I'd found a way to avoid the sales quotas and corporate pressures. But soon, I realized the challenges were just as significant, albeit in different ways. My schedule became even more demanding. I trained clients from 4:15 a.m. to 12 p.m., took a short break, and then returned for evening sessions from 3:30 p.m. to 8:30 p.m. My Fridays were slightly shorter, but I still worked Saturdays.

I told myself this pace was temporary, that I was building something worthwhile. And I was—but at what cost? My relationships suffered, my health deteriorated, and I found myself questioning whether this was sustainable. I loved training, but I couldn't keep up the relentless pace.

These experiences shaped my approach when I founded Precision Training. I realized that growth didn't have to come at the expense of well-being. My goal became creating an environment where trainers could thrive—professionally and personally—without sacrificing their health or happiness.

*A System That Works Against Trainers*

The challenges trainers face are often systemic. In many gyms, trainers are treated as commodities rather than professionals. Sales goals are set without regard for experience or capacity. Accountability is minimal. Workloads are unsustainable. And the profession itself offers little in the way of mentorship or guidance.

I've seen the fallout of this approach firsthand:

- Trainers scrolling through their phones during sessions or disengaging entirely.
- Inappropriate behavior, from dressing unprofessionally to discussing personal lives with clients.
- Overstepping professional boundaries by offering advice on medications or medical diagnoses.
- Trainers leaving within 60-90 days, sending a message to potential clients that the gym—and the trainers themselves—can't be trusted to stay or remain committed.

These behaviors don't just reflect poorly on individual trainers—they erode trust in the profession as a whole. At Precision Training, I've worked to create a culture that sets a higher standard. We focus on professionalism, accountability, and mutual support. Our trainers know they're part of a team, and that team is invested in their growth.

### BUILDING A WIN-WIN CULTURE

When I first opened my gym in 2016, hiring or mentoring trainers wasn't even on my radar. My sole focus was paying my mortgage and helping clients achieve their goals. But as my business grew, so did the demands on my time. A year and a half later, my mindset shifted from, *"I don't need help,"* to, *"I need a team I can trust, so I can see my family."*

This realization became the foundation for building Precision Training's win-win culture, inspired by Stephen Covey's principle of mutual benefit. The system we've developed prioritizes the success of both trainers and clients, creating an environment where no one's progress comes at someone else's expense.

For trainers, this meant creating a structure that alleviates the stress of taking a break—whether it's for a vacation, a personal matter, or a weekend course to further their education. In many gym environments, the impact of taking time off is felt before trainers even leave. Clients feel the disruption, sessions go unfulfilled, and income takes a hit. At Precision Training, we wanted to change that dynamic by building systems that allow trainers to take time off without the emotional and financial strain as well as taking into account professional benefits that everyone should have access to.

These include:

- **Fair Compensation:** Trainers are paid appropriately for their time, effort, and expertise—not just the hours they log.
- **PTO and Benefits:** Every team member has at least 40 hours of paid time off, access to health insurance, and retirement savings options.
- **Time-Off Support:** When trainers need time away, their sessions are distributed across the team. This ensures clients feel supported and continuity is maintained, allowing trainers to step away without guilt or fear of letting anyone down.

- **Accountability and Development:** Regular feedback sessions and opportunities for professional growth help trainers refine their skills and stay engaged.

For clients, this win-win culture ensures a seamless and supportive experience, no matter the circumstances. From day one, every new client at Precision Training embarks on a comprehensive onboarding process that sets the foundation for their long-term success with us. This includes personalized assessments, structured accountability, and consistent access to a team that is fully invested in their growth.

- **Precision Assessment:** Our method to identify each person's unique physiological starting point.
    - **60–75 Minute 1-on-1 Session:** A personalized introduction with one of our expert trainers.
    - **3D Body Scan:** To gather accurate biometric data and track progress over time.
    - **Comprehensive Movement Screening:** Analyzing joint range of motion, mechanical awareness, stability, and muscle flexibility.
    - **Core Activation & Bracing Awareness Check:** To ensure clients understand how to stabilize effectively.
    - **Cardiovascular Assessment:** Tailored to their fitness level and goals.
- **Personalized Nutrition Plan:** Built around their lifestyle, preferences, and needs.

- **Accountability Coach:** To provide ongoing support and motivation.
- **Workouts with a Trainer 3x Per Week:** Offering the guidance and structure they need to thrive.

The Precision Training system is designed to empower clients with the tools, insights, and encouragement they need to make sustainable progress. Even when their primary trainer is unavailable, the continuity built into the program ensures they feel cared for, supported, and on track toward their goals.

*Why It Matters*

This win-win mindset transforms more than just the professional lives of trainers—it redefines the client experience, fostering a culture of growth, trust, and mutual support where everyone thrives. When trainers are empowered to prioritize their well-being, they show up energized, focused, and fully committed to their clients' success. Clients, in turn, benefit from personalized care and continuity, knowing they are supported by a system that values progress, not just transactions. By raising the bar for how trainers and clients are treated, this approach elevates the entire industry, proving that sustainable success doesn't come at the expense of anyone's well-being.

Still, even within a supportive environment, the demands of the fitness profession don't vanish—they require intentionality, resilience, and a commitment to balance.

Showing up for yourself as a coach isn't a luxury; it's a necessity. Without prioritizing your own well-being, burnout becomes inevitable, and your ability to serve others diminishes. So how do you navigate the weight of these responsibilities while fostering your own growth and fulfillment? The answer lies in cultivating habits and mindsets that empower you to sustain your passion and purpose for the long haul. Let's explore the lessons learned from these challenges and how they shape a healthier, more sustainable path forward.

## LESSONS LEARNED THE HARD WAY: SHOWING UP FOR YOURSELF

One of the most profound lessons I've learned as a coach is this: you can't pour from an empty cup. Your ability to show up for your clients—energized, present, and effective—begins with showing up for yourself. But what does "showing up for yourself" really mean in a profession that revolves around others? Self-care in the fitness industry often defaults to physical health—trainers are typically great at staying active, eating well, and maintaining a certain appearance. But true self-care goes deeper. It's about more than just staying fit—it's about building a foundation of habits, routines, and a clear sense of purpose that keeps you grounded and able to handle the physical, emotional, and mental challenges of coaching day in and day out. To keep yourself above water (so to speak) takes intentional work cultivating habits, mindsets, and systems that prioritize your well-being without compromising your commitment to your clients. It can't be understated that rest isn't a reward for hard work—it's a requirement for longevity.

Take **rest** seriously. Whether it's a dedicated afternoon each week or a vacation you actually unplug for, rest helps you recharge and return with clarity. **Reflection** is equally important. The emotional energy absorbed from clients can build up, and processing it regularly prevents burnout. Don't overlook basic recovery strategies either: prioritize quality sleep, hydration, and nutrition—not just for peak performance but for long-term health and sustainability.

But showing up for yourself isn't just about rest—it's about managing your energy output and work capacity in a sustainable way. A common trap in the fitness industry is equating success with an overpacked schedule, but more clients and busier days don't always translate to better outcomes. Success isn't about cramming everything into your schedule—it's about finding a rhythm that allows you to consistently show up at your best, even in a new or unpredictable environment. While you can't always control when your toughest sessions will fall, you can focus on what's within your reach: preparing, recovering, and finding small ways to recharge throughout the day. Taking even five minutes between sessions to breathe, hydrate, or reflect can dramatically improve your presence and effectiveness for your following sessions. Simple practices, like staying properly fueled, taking a quick walk to reset your mind, or carving out non-negotiable recovery/reflection time for yourself each week, can make all the difference in sustaining your physical, mental, and emotional energy as well as staying connected to your purpose as a trainer.

Take a moment to reflect:

- Are you proud of the relationships you've built and the values you embody as a coach?
- Are you maintaining boundaries that protect your energy and time?
- Are you improving your skills and mindset each year?

These questions can help you redefine success on your terms, making it both fulfilling and achievable.

Equally critical is building a strong support system. Navigating the challenges of the fitness industry isn't something you should face alone. Yet, in an industry often dominated by lone-wolf mentalities, finding like-minded professionals can feel daunting. For me, the difference came from seeking out growth-minded peers beyond my immediate environment—through weekend courses, professional networks, and even reaching out to coaches who shared my hunger for development on social media. As Craig Groeschel wisely said, *"Culture is a combination of what you create and what you allow."* By intentionally building connections with those who aligned with my values and vision, I found accountability, encouragement, and perspective to stay focused on what mattered most.

Finally, remember that you are more than just a trainer— you are a leader. Your clients don't just listen to what you say and watch what you demo; they observe how you live. When you're facing struggles, that's your opportunity to model resilience, balance, and growth. You can inspire them to do the same. Showing your clients how you navigate challenges with integrity and perseverance can be one of the most impactful lessons you share.

By prioritizing yourself—your health, your growth, your well-being—you don't just elevate your coaching. You create an experience that resonates with your clients, helping them see the power of commitment and balance in their own lives.

*Reflection Exercises*

1. **Identify Stressors:** Take five minutes to write down the biggest stressors in your career right now. Be honest with yourself. What's consistently draining your energy or holding you back from being your best? Whether it's a packed schedule, unclear boundaries, or feelings of self-doubt, identifying these stressors is the first step toward addressing them.
2. **Set Boundaries:** Choose one way to protect your time, energy, or mental health this week. It might mean blocking off a specific time for yourself, saying "no" to something you'd normally say "yes" to, or creating a clear separation between work and personal life. Boundaries aren't limitations—they're safeguards for your well-being and effectiveness.

3. **Seek Support:** Reflect on an area in your career where you feel stuck or could benefit from guidance. Is it technical knowledge, client communication, time management, or something else? Once you've identified it, then take intentional action—reach out to a colleague for their perspective, join a professional network to broaden your connections, or connect with a trusted mentor who can offer seasoned advice. Growth often thrives in community, and leaning into the collective wisdom of others can unlock new insights and opportunities. Remember, isolation stifles growth, but collaboration and seeking support pave the way for developing resilience and making progress.

Each of these exercises is designed to help you take small but meaningful steps toward reclaiming control over your career and well-being. By making reflection and intentional action a regular practice, you'll build the resilience and clarity needed to thrive in both your personal and professional life.

*Chapter Summary*

The fitness industry challenges you to give your best to others, but true success begins with the choices you make to sustain yourself. By prioritizing boundaries, leaning on support systems, and committing to meaningful growth, you create a career that thrives without sacrifice. Your well-being sets the stage for the energy, focus, and empathy you bring to each client. When you take care of yourself, you lead by example, showing your clients that true strength is found in balance, consistency, and the courage to prioritize what matters most. Every action you take to support your own growth elevates not just your coaching, but the lives of those you're privileged to guide.

7

# THE COACH'S LEGACY

Coaching isn't just about what happens in the gym—it's about the lasting influence you leave on your clients, your team, and the industry as a whole. Your legacy as a coach isn't determined by how much money you make, the number of transformations you post on social media, the number of followers you have on social media, or the accolades you earn over time. Your legacy as a coach will be defined by the relationships you built, and how you managed them over time.

Your influence as a coach extends far beyond the walls of the gym. Whether it's helping a client develop resilience that they carry into their career or modeling empathy that encourages them to deepen their role in relationships, the ripple effect of your work often reaches places you'll never see. This chapter is about embracing that ripple effect, owning the responsibility of your influence, and understanding the honor and tremendous privilege of shaping lives through coaching.

## TRUST AS THE FOUNDATION OF LEGACY

At the heart of every meaningful coaching relationship lies one essential element: trust. As mentioned previously, without trust, even the most knowledgeable trainer will fail to connect. Trust allows clients to open up, take risks, and push past their doubts. It is the foundation of any relationship, and there's always a cost involved to get something you want. Trust isn't given, it's earned, and once it's earned, it's often tested in unexpected ways.

One of my longest-standing clients taught me this lesson early in my career. After training together for about a month, she walked into the gym and handed me her food journal. It was filled with items like pizza, brownies, and ice cream. My initial reaction was a mix of judgment and frustration. I didn't need to say much because my disapproval was written all over my face. She felt it immediately, and it broke the trust we'd been building. Moments later, she walked out of the gym, leaving me stunned and questioning everything.

I had failed her. I had failed to create a space where she felt safe sharing her struggles. My focus had been on the "what"—what she ate, what she logged—not the "why" behind her choices or the courage it took to be honest with me. After a lot of reflection and advice from a mentor, I called her to apologize. It wasn't easy, because part of me still thought she was wrong for eating foods that would take her further away from her goals. But, another part of me realized I'd missed the bigger picture. She was a month into training, and her food choices were just starting to surface. She didn't share her journal because she was resisting the nutrition plan I had introduced weeks prior. She shared it because she had struggled with food her entire life. She wanted help, not judgment. My visceral reaction was centered on her actions, rather than understanding her perspective or supporting her vulnerability.

That phone call became a turning point for both of us. I had to step outside my bias and let go of the perfection I thought was required for success. She, on the other hand, needed a coach who wouldn't see her missteps as failures, but as part of a battle she'd been fighting for decades. In that moment, I realized coaching wasn't just about guiding physical transformation—it was about standing beside someone as they faced their deepest challenges with the confidence that you're in their corner to watch them win.

She returned to training shortly thereafter, and over time, she achieved incredible feats—hiking some of the most challenging treks in the world and inspiring her husband to join her fitness journey. That experience reminded me that trust isn't just about what we say; it's about how we make people feel, how we listen, and how we respond in the moments that matter most.

## THE RIPPLE EFFECT OF RELATIONSHIPS

The impact of your coaching doesn't stop with the client in front of you. The lessons you teach often ripple outward into their families, communities, and workplaces. A client who builds confidence in the gym may find themselves standing taller in the boardroom. A client who learns resilience in training may show that same determination when facing challenges in their personal life.

When you approach coaching with the mindset of leaving a legacy, you begin to see every session as part of a bigger picture. You're not just helping clients lift weights or lose pounds—you're equipping them with tools they can carry into every aspect of their lives.

This ripple effect also applies to your influence on other trainers. By modeling professionalism, empathy, and intentionality, you raise the bar for those around you. Your legacy isn't just about your clients—it's about the standard you set for the industry. Every action, every conversation, and every example you set contributes to this ripple effect. By holding yourself to a higher standard, you inspire others to do the same, creating a culture where growth and excellence become the norm, not the exception.

## COLLABORATIVE PRECISION

Great coaches understand that their impact extends far beyond the individual client. Every choice you make—every habit you build, every standard you set—ripples outward, shaping the broader environment and culture of those you influence. This is where your values as a leader come into play. At Precision Training, one of our core values is *collaborative precision*—the belief that excellence isn't a solo act; it's a shared pursuit built on trust, alignment, and intentionality.

As a coach, your precision is in the details: whether it's refining a client's form or thoughtfully following up on a question they asked last week, the care you put into planning a session, the way you listen to a client's concerns, the encouragement you offer when they doubt themselves. When you model collaboration—working with teammates, seeking input, and celebrating shared wins—you help to create an environment where growth and trust flourish. Clients notice this culture. It builds their confidence not just in you, but in the entire experience you've created for them.

Your leadership sets the tone. If you bring intentionality to your interactions and consistency to your actions, you show others what's possible. You prove that transformation isn't just about physical change—it's about fostering an environment where everyone, from clients to team members, feels empowered to grow together. A coach who lives by their values isn't just inspiring—they're magnetic. They don't just guide workouts; they draw others toward excellence through their authenticity and example.

Collaborative precision also means being open to the contributions of others. Whether it's learning from a teammate, taking feedback from a client, or mentoring a younger trainer, great leaders recognize that progress happens together. Your ability to elevate others—to amplify their strengths, and align their efforts toward shared goals—is what transforms good coaching into meaningful leadership.

The habits, values, and presence you embody as a coach will outlive the sessions you lead. Clients will carry the lessons you've taught them into their lives. Your team will carry forward the standards you've modeled in their interactions. The culture you've created will continue to inspire long after you've stepped away from the gym floor, shaping not just the present but the future of those who follow in your footsteps. This is the essence of your legacy: the way you've shown up for others, not just in moments of triumph but in the quiet, consistent actions that shape trust, growth, and connection over time.

## DEVELOPING YOUR CORE VALUES

The lasting impact of your coaching—on clients, teammates, and the broader culture you influence—begins with the values that guide you. Collaborative precision thrives when coaches lead with clarity and authenticity, but defining your core values is the first step. These values serve as the foundation for every decision, interaction, and habit you build, shaping the trust and alignment that inspire growth in those around you.

While many coaches operate with an intuitive sense of their values, taking the time to identify, refine, and live by them is what transforms good intentions into purposeful leadership. This process of defining your core values not only deepens your understanding of yourself but also strengthens the culture of excellence and trust you're building.

One effective way to clarify your values is through a value-sorting activity—a reflective exercise that narrows down what matters most to you and ensures your actions align with your beliefs. Here's how to get started:

*1. Create a List of Values:*

Start with a broad list of potential values—many online resources and tools offer value-sorting activities you can use. Examples of values might include integrity, growth, empathy, creativity, or service. Write down as many as resonate with you.

*2. Sort and Prioritize:*

- Narrow your list to 10–15 values that feel most significant to you.
- Rank these values in order of importance, focusing on the top five that truly represent your core principles. These are the non-negotiables that guide your decisions and behavior.

*3. Reflect on Alignment:*

For each of your top five values, think about moments in your life when these values were evident. Ask yourself:

- When have I felt most aligned with this value?

- How does this value influence my approach to coaching and leadership?

### 4. Test for Alignment:

Consider how your actions and decisions align with your values. Are there areas where your actions fall short? If so, what changes can you make to live more authentically according to your values?

## FROM VALUES TO LEGACY

Identifying your core values is just the beginning. To build a coaching legacy that endures, those values must shape your daily decisions, actions, and relationships. When consistently applied, your values become the foundation for the trust, impact, and growth you bring to your clients and your leadership.

The following reflection exercises are designed to bridge the gap between identifying your values and living them with intention. By connecting your guiding principles to specific actions, you can ensure that your values are the cornerstone of your coaching legacy.

### *Reflection Exercises*

Your legacy as a coach is shaped by the intentional steps you take every day. These exercises are designed to help you reflect on your values, assess your impact, and set a clear vision for the leader you aspire to be. Take your time with each question—it's through this kind of reflection that true growth begins.

1. **Define Your Core Values**

Spend 10 minutes reflecting on how your top values are evident in your actions, decisions, and interactions with clients and colleagues.

- Are there moments where your actions don't fully align with your intentions?
- What specific steps can you take to better live out these values each day?

2. **Assess Your Ripple Effect**

Consider the broader impact of your coaching—the ripple effect you create in the lives of others.

- What type of influence are you currently having on your clients, your team, and your community?
- Does your impact reflect the values you outlined in the previous exercise? If not, what adjustments can you make to bring your ripple effect in line with your intentions?

3. **Your Leadership Vision**

Picture yourself five years from now, overhearing a colleague describing your leadership to someone else.

- What words do you hope they use to describe you?
- Does that vision excite, challenge, or even scare you?
- What habits, mindsets, or systems need to change today to bring that vision to life?

***Chapter Summary: A Legacy of Trust and Influence***

Your influence as a coach stretches far beyond the gym walls—it lives in the ripple effects of your choices, your values, and your presence. Every moment, every interaction, and every habit you cultivate contributes to the story of your legacy. As the saying goes:

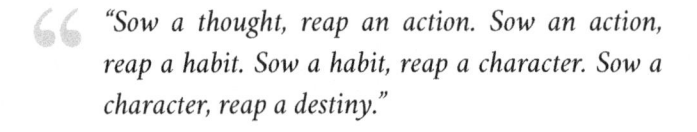

> *"Sow a thought, reap an action. Sow an action, reap a habit. Sow a habit, reap a character. Sow a character, reap a destiny."*

Coaching isn't just a career—it's a calling, a privilege to shape lives and leave the world better than you found it. The confidence you help a client discover can transform their sense of self. The mentorship you offer a fellow trainer can elevate the next generation of leaders. The culture you create in your gym can inspire trust, growth, and community. Every session, every conversation, and every act of trust is a building block in the legacy you leave behind.

This work is bigger than you, but it begins with you. Your legacy isn't defined by perfection—it's defined by consistency, intention, and the courage to show up fully each day. Inspire others not just through what you do, but through the way you live—with purpose, resilience, and hope.

This is the responsibility—and the privilege—of being a coach. Embrace it. Own it. And let every action you take ripple outward as a force for transformation.

# EPILOGUE: THE JOURNEY AHEAD

As you've worked through this book, I hope you've begun to embrace a deeper philosophy of coaching: one that values people over numbers and places connection at the core of everything you do. Coaching involves more than simply delivering workouts or guiding clients toward goals. It demands an approach that seeks to build trust at the client's pace, be respectful of the client's needs, and share the commitment and responsibility toward growth.

We've only scratched the surface of what it means to observe movement with precision, adapt in real time, and craft sessions that reflect not only your expertise but also your clients' unique needs and circumstances. These pages are a foundation, but the true depth of learning happens in the moments you share with your clients. Each session is an opportunity to refine your craft, learn from experience, and grow alongside those you coach.

The tools you've gained require effort and intentionality to master. They are not fixed or static but evolve as you do—shaped by the challenges you face and the lessons you learn. Just as you ask your clients to commit to their progress, you must hold yourself to the same standard—continuously raising the bar and striving for excellence in every aspect of your coaching.

## A VISION FOR THE FUTURE

Imagine each session as a space where clients feel seen, understood, and motivated to become their best selves. They leave your care not just physically stronger but with a renewed sense of confidence and purpose, assured in their trust of your judgment and uplifted by the unwavering support of a coach who genuinely believes in their potential.

Imagine yourself guiding a first-time client through their initial steps with patience and encouragement. Envision the satisfaction of challenging a seasoned athlete to push beyond their limits while maintaining trust and connection. See yourself adapting seamlessly for a client recovering from injury, offering them the tools to rebuild strength and resilience.

This isn't a dream reserved for the future—it's a reality you can create. When you approach each session with curiosity, empathy, and intention, you inspire trust and cultivate lasting transformation. It's a process built on consistency and the courage to lead with purpose, regardless of the challenges you face.

## A CALL TO ACTION

Transformation begins with a single, intentional step. Start today by selecting one principle from this book and committing to its application. Whether it's refining your ability to observe movement, tailoring your approach based on what you learn in real time, identifying and aligning with your core values, or asking a question that deepens your understanding of your client's needs and goals, each action lays the foundation for lasting growth.

Reflect on your practice and consider:

- What's one area of my coaching that needs immediate attention?
- How can I create a better experience for my clients this week?

Write your thoughts down and revisit them often. Let these reflections become a roadmap for your growth. True progress doesn't require perfection—it's built on consistency, resilience, and the willingness to adapt.

## LOOKING AHEAD

The principles you've explored here mark the start of a transformative journey in your career. They've equipped you with a foundation to build upon, but they are only the beginning. In the next installment, we'll dive into the art and science of program design—an essential skill that forms the backbone of effective coaching.

You'll learn how to create individualized, purposeful plans that align with your clients' goals and deliver measurable results. From structuring progressions and balancing recovery to creating adaptable systems for real-world application, program design is the bridge between assessment and achievement. It's the process where data and creativity converge to create training plans that are not only effective but also deeply aligned with each client's unique goals and needs. Mastering this skill enables you to craft solutions that guide clients through each phase of their journey while reinforcing the trust they place in your expertise.

As you move forward, remember that coaching mastery is never static. It's a continuous evolution, fueled by curiosity and the drive to improve. Every new skill builds upon the last, creating a career that is both fulfilling and impactful. The path ahead will challenge you, but it will also reward you in ways you can't yet imagine.

Embrace the journey. Pursue growth relentlessly. And take pride in the knowledge that each step forward enriches not just your practice but the lives of those you coach.

## A CLOSING THOUGHT

Your impact matters. You're more than a trainer—you're a guide, a mentor, and a catalyst for transformation. Your clients come to you because they trust you to help them uncover their potential and achieve goals they once thought were impossible. Every session is an opportunity to guide them toward their aspirations while revealing strengths they never knew they had.

Your work and the time you put into developing yourself matter. The dedication you bring to your own growth directly shapes the lives of your clients, and the trust they place in you reflects that commitment. Coaching is an act of service—a blend of skill and care that creates lasting change.

The choices you make—to adapt, to listen, to lead with intention—shape not only the trajectory of your clients' journeys but also your own legacy as a coach. Every session is an opportunity to connect, empower, and inspire.

So, commit to growth. Commit to your clients. Commit to the lifelong pursuit of excellence that makes this career so meaningful. Show up not just to lead workouts but to change lives. Keep refining, keep learning, and never lose sight of why you started.

# REFERENCES

Covey, S. R. (1989). *The 7 habits of highly effective people: Powerful lessons in personal change.* Free Press.

AhaSlides. (2024). Celebrating small wins: How little victories boost happiness and productivity. Retrieved from https://ahaslides.com/blog/celebrating-small-wins

Psychology Today. (2024). From small steps to big wins: The importance of celebrating accomplishments. Retrieved from https://www.psychologytoday.com/us/blog/empower-your-mind/202406/from-small-steps-to-big-wins-the-importance-of-celebrating

Heath, C., & Heath, D. (2013). Decisive: How to make better choices in life and work. Crown Business.

Covey, S. R. (1994). First things first. Simon & Schuster.

Groeschel, C. (2014). *IT: How churches and leaders can get it and keep it.* Zondervan.

Holiday, R. (2016). *Ego is the enemy.* Portfolio.

Maxwell, J. C. (1998). *The 21 irrefutable laws of leadership: Follow them and people will follow you.* Thomas Nelson.